THE UNINTENTIONAL IMMIGRANT

*From Aspiring Surgeon
to Undercover Operative*

Jorge H. DeNapoli

The Unintentional Immigrant: From Aspiring Surgeon to Undercover Operative. Copyright © 2019 Jorge H. DeNapoli. Produced and printed by Stillwater River Publications. All rights reserved. Written and produced in the United States of America. This book may not be reproduced or sold in any form without the expressed, written permission of the authors and publisher.
Visit our website at www.StillwaterPress.com for more information.

First Stillwater River Publications Edition 2019.

ISBN-10: 1-950339-16-5
ISBN-13: 978-1-950339-16-7

1 2 3 4 5 6 7 8 9 10

Written by Jorge H. DeNapoli.
Cover design by Dawn M. Porter.

Published by Stillwater River Publications, Pawtucket, RI, USA.

I dedicate this book to my late wife Dolores,
the catalytic force that changed the course of my life,
and who shared my turbulent journey
making our bond stronger
with every road we traveled.

To my children:
Jorge Alan, aka Tiki; Deirdre, and Melissa.

To my grandchildren.

And in memory of Jorge Spencer, beloved son,
our *Gentle Giant,* smiling to us from Heaven.

Together, they symbolize the dream
of family happiness.

This is the story of my life, as accurately portrayed as memory allows. I have changed the names of some people to ensure their privacy. I have also deliberately distorted the particulars of some events or situations so that resemblances to real life happenings are obscured, purely for the protection, safety, and confidentiality of its participants.

"A person often meets his destiny on the road he took to avoid it"

~Jean de La Fountaine (1621–1695)

TABLE OF CONTENTS

ACKNOWLEDGMENTS

I am gratefully indebted to my teacher and friend Priscilla Dullea who nurtured me through creative writing classes, stood by my side chapter after chapter challenging my writing skills, correcting my prose, and actually telling me where to put the commas.

Thanks to my beta-readers of the Rockingham Writers Group in Salem, New Hampshire, especially Susan Piazza, Barbara Prolman, Dan Dancer, Brian Sullivan and Ron Penczak, for their positive critical advise and encouragement.

To Kate Victory Hannisian of Blue Pencil Consulting, for her fine editing and book proposal work, and sound advice in the format of my book.

Most appreciative to author Satin Russell, friend and fellow member at the Newburyport Writers Group, for her unselfish advice and guidance in the publishing process.

I would especially like to thank my grandson Chandler P. Dunn, M.S. in computer science, for his invaluable help with my predicaments in the cyber arena.

Finally, to my family and all my friends who constantly encourage me to put in writing my adventurous journey in life.

PROLOGUE

The morose calmness of that balmy late afternoon in the Indian summer of 1980 was suddenly broken by the ringing of my office telephone. My office manager Patricia White had left moments before, so after several rings I responded to the call that unbeknown to me, would eventually submerge my life in an intriguing and risky double existence for years to come.

I identified myself when answering.

"Doctor DeNapoli... my name is Mike. I'm calling from Washington," the voice continued. "I'm a special U.S. government agent for the Office of Strategic Information." *Interesting,* I thought. *Is this a prank?*

Mike continued with an explanation of the purpose of his call. "I'll be traveling to Lowell and would like to meet with you."

The call sparked my interest. It surprised and intrigued me. Clouds of doubt glutted my mind. It sounded like a legitimate proposal but maybe it was a friend pulling my leg? Or perhaps a patient with delusional ideas? I kept listening.

"Could we meet on Thursday evening? At Pollard's Restaurant on Middle Street? We could have a coffee there. I will recognize you: we have already done a background profile." *Really*? I was suspicious, but more intrigued.

"I have office hours until six. Will seven be alright?" Mike agreed.

Two days later I drove from my home in the town of Andover to Lowell, a mid-size city in northeastern Massachusetts. I was still skeptical about the nature of this meeting. Skeptical, but curious.

Mike, a tall athletic-looking man in his early forties, approached me as soon as I entered the restaurant. He wore a well-tailored business suit.

Once we sat down with our coffees, I listened intently as Mike told me all about myself. I became aware that a full dossier had been compiled of my entire life. Family, acquaintances, activities, and professional achievements had been thoroughly investigated. To my relief, the only thing he didn't mention was my sexual peccadilloes. A few times, as detail after detail unfolded, I thought I wouldn't be able to keep from spitting coffee across the table in surprise, ruining Mike's white shirt. It's a strange feeling to have the lid peeled off your life like that. You begin to wonder if they know more about you than you do, but I somehow managed to shake off the surreal weirdness of it all as Mike continued to talk. He said that I interested the government both because of my professional status and my predilection for international travel.

My frequent travels to attend scientific conferences, give lectures, visit friends or just vacation wouldn't arouse any suspicion. During these trips I would serve the country by working for the Office of Strategic Information (OSI) as a courier in the *Dogwood Chain.*

This service had been established during World War II in Istanbul, Turkey, by a Czechoslovakian engineer and businessman known by the code name *Dogwood.* Its purpose was the gathering of intelligence information to be transmitted to the Central Command in Washington, D.C. During the post WWII era, and most probably to the present day, they recruited a significant but unknown number of American citizens for voluntary participation in this expanded chain. They were businessmen, professionals, entertainers, artists, and world travelers, who, because of their status and their opportunity to visit strategic countries all around the world, could collect specifically requested information without arousing suspicion. Their mission was to memorize, record, or photograph such information and produce analytical reports for the Office of Strategic Information through a designated agent.

They had selected me on the recommendation of a Washington official connected to a mutual friend's earlier political campaign. I learned that as an operative I should never expect any feedback on how the completion of my assignments helped to ensure the security of the country or impact any specific occurrence. Mike would be my contact person.

I was apprehensive, but at the same time intrigued and excited at the prospect of participating in such an undercover adventure. I did not like to avoid a good challenge.

Previous missteps in my younger years resulting from impulsive decisions had taught me to analyze and evaluate complex or unusual proposals or situations with exhaustive caution. So that's what I set out to do.

Following my initial meeting with Mike, I researched government books and documents, obtained information from my contacts in high-level positions in Boston and Bethesda, Maryland, and attended private meetings with Washington officials to acquire information that was kept from general knowledge. I learned that the Office of Strategic Information (OSI) was an obscure branch of the Office of Strategic Services (OSS) created by President Franklin D. Roosevelt in June 1941, just prior to the United States' entry into World War II. It was similar in form to the British MI-8 intelligence group (closed in 1929).

The OSS operated from different sites, internally designated as areas A, B, C and F, which were located in Bethesda and Washington, D.C. These offices served various purposes in clandestine intelligence. The OSI was based in area F, but there is no paper trail that OSI ever existed. Even so, the Dogwood

Chain, known to insiders as *"civilian para-marines,"* continued undercover operations post WWII after the OSS dissolved. In 1945, the War Department took over the Secret Intelligence (SI) and counterespionage (X2) and combined them to create the Strategic Central Service Unit that was renamed a year later as the Central Intelligence Group reporting directly to President Harry Truman. This unit was the precursor to today's Central Intelligence Agency (CIA). The OSI survived all these changes and continued to operate in the shadows. It was only after September 11, 2001 that President George W. Bush would officially create a *new* Office of Strategic Information.

I had compiled sufficient data to reach a reasonable decision. If I were to participate in this clandestine adventure, I had to undergo a security clearance investigation and swear complete secrecy. It would take months for me to finalize my decision. I had an outgoing personality, but I could not picture myself as an undercover operative leading a secret double life. *I am no James Bond*, I had concluded. I was also interested to know what other factors had played a role in my selection. I wanted my wife to share in the decision. However, when I asked to Mike about letting my wife in on the plan, he strongly objected. "The wife should never know. Women tend to confide in their girlfriends, and besides, you can never predict what the outcome of any marriage might be. It's always safer for the wife or close family members not to know."

I did not entirely agree with his recommendations, but unfortunately, if I was going to participate, I had no say in the matter. Mike gave me a telephone number to memorize for when I was ready to contact him about my decision.

For weeks I pondered my next move. I wanted to be of service to my adopted country but did not want to enter a situation from which there might be no way out. I would have to decide alone, and for my own reasons.

CHAPTER ONE

My journey to the Northern Hemisphere started long ago when I stood, suitcase in hand, full of the thrill of adventure. The prospect of my first long-distance flight charged me with anticipation. It was 1956 and I felt relieved to be leaving Buenos Aires. Argentina's recent political life had been volatile. Juan Peron had been deposed by the military less than six months before, and yet the insecurity of governmental upheaval persisted.

Before any more turmoil erupted I would be gone, saved from possible conscripted participation in the army. I was concerned with my own plans, dreaming of an exuberant future, and determined to muster the bravado to step into it. It was easy to be brave; I wasn't leaving my native land forever.

My confidence welled-up from the future I imagined, returning as my own conquering hero, well credentialed and ready to open my surgical practice. Buenos Aires was *home*; so it would be again. My ticket represented not just a plane trip, but access to the American internship that would place me at the cutting edge of the eminent surgical career I envisioned. Keeping my *someday* in mind focused me, generating and renewing the energy that created my buoyancy.

My parents had not been so much politically naïve as cautious. They believed ambition, determination, and sweat were the best tools of success, paying attention to the government's machinations, but refraining from becoming involved in political activism. They put their energy into realizing personal goals, while the hope of creating a perfect world seemed to them delusional, and dangerous. They and their circle of friends felt their first duty was to family. To perform individually as well as their capabilities ordained was the best plan. They were grounded in the certainty that this was the path to success and security. Their attitude and example were their legacy.

The new military government went about overseeing the country's business. Our family avoided discussing how stable their regime would prove to be. They believed in the possibility of an Argentinean democracy and maintained optimism about Argentina's prosperity, but they counted on nothing other than their own ingenuity. They lived in the present, prudently minding their own business, yet with enough foresight to visualize what could come next. I had absorbed the ethics of; *dream, plan, do*; appreciate the place of each, but orient toward doing. Possibility informed my choices, it was a style that had worked well for me, so far.

Now I had at last arrived at the starting point. I was more than ready when the twin- engine, propeller-driven Convair rolled up to the terminal at Ezeiza Airport, a forty-five-minute drive from Buenos Aires. I said my goodbyes to my parents, brother and sister. There were tears of concern in my mother's eyes. With a reassuring smile from my father, I scrambled up the stairs eagerly, nodded to the flight attendant, scanned the passenger deck, and found my window seat. Full of an ebullient sense of destiny, I stowed my jacket and settled in.

It would be a long flight. I felt the rhythmic droning of the plane's engines vibrating through my bones, tolerable only because it meant my future was under way. We flew long hours over the Brazilian forest at just 12,000 feet; increasing my awareness of my journey's scope and the boldness of flying over such an immense jungle. Argentina is a large country, but it pales in comparison to the vastness of Brazil.

After several hours, we landed in Belem, Brazil, to re-fuel. At the time it was a smalltown embracing the coast, carved into the smallest fringe of encroaching jungle. While the plane was serviced, we had a chance to stretch our stiff muscles and quench our thirst. Then I re-boarded the plane, no longer a nov-ice flier. The rest of the flight alternated over land and water. I could only guess what part of the world we flew over as each appeared and disappeared far below. The enormity of the jour-ney underscored my own insignificance as we traveled from one hemisphere into another, and from my past life into my future.

The Convair aircraft taxied to a jerky stop on the tarmac at Miami International Airport. My stomach lurched along with the bouncing tires.

I had left the political turmoil of post-Peron's Argentina after earning a medical degree, traveling to more promising skies for an internship prior to seeking specialized training in surgery.

As I stepped onto United States soil, I was conflicted as to what I should do: kiss the ground as I had seen someone do in the movies, or just follow the group into the terminal? I chose the latter.

With the other passengers, I walked through a maze of wide, glass-lined corridors until we reached the Immigration Hall. People waited in lines in front of the booths. Dressed in my two-piece suit I blended unnoticed with men in their business attire. Women wore light-colored dresses and attractive accessories. When my turn came, the immigration officer greeted me with a smile.

"Mr. Jorge DeNapoli, welcome to the United States," he said as he stamped my passport.

The imprint read, "Admitted – February 15, 1956."

I returned the smile, not as a polite gesture, but in response to the officer's mispronunciation of my name. I thought to myself, *Welcome to the English-speaking world.*

I moved on to search for my luggage. I'd brought only one suitcase with my clothes, photographs, memory tokens from my natal land, and my medical diploma. Everything else was left behind: my medical books, lots of memorabilia, and all my family.

After reuniting with my luggage, I began exploring the large terminal looking for the Eastern Airlines ticket counter. My ticket showed that they would transport me to my final destination, New York City. Although ecstatic to have fulfilled my young man's notion of coming to the States, I was also apprehensive and even somewhat frightened. I remember thinking, *I am not alone. My confidence and youthful determination are my companions.*

And also your poor English, my apprehension had taunted. I approached a couple of airport employees, but they couldn't understand me. Likewise, I had no idea what they said in return. So much for the English courses taken at home! I eventually gave up and showed them my airline ticket and was directed to the Eastern counter. I was fortunate that one of the clerks spoke Spanish and I was able to board the plane without further difficulty.

The flight to New York was uneventful, but by then I was so weary it would have taken a great deal to bother me. What a long way I had come, not just in terms of miles traveled, but in terms of how much of my former life had been jettisoned in the plane's wake.

It was cold, windy, and snowing when we left the plane at Idlewild International Airport in New York. I was no stranger to cold weather. Winter temperatures in Buenos Aires would frequently drop to the below-freezing mark. But snow was a new experience. New York was greeting my arrival with a white carpet of fresh snow. At the plane's exit door, the flight attendant motioned to me to put on the winter coat I carried over my arm. I then climbed down the rolled-up staircase and stepped on the soft white powder covering the dirty ugliness of the tarmac.

My poetic entrance to the terminal was sort lived. It was a busy place. Dozens of travelers hurried along, and there were a multitude of signs posted, and blaring messages I couldn't understand. At last, I spotted one that said, "Taxi."

While walking toward it, I heard a skycap speaking my language. I hurried after him and asked how to get to the city.

"A taxi all the way into the city will be very expensive. Take the bus," the skycap advised, grabbing me by the arm. "Come with me."

We walked almost to the other side of the large hall, where the skycap pointed to the bus ticket office. "This bus will drop you off in Manhattan at the 34th Street Station. From there you can take a taxi to your destination," he said.

Tired, I sat on a bench in the small waiting room of the bus station. My suitcase, storehouse of all my possessions, rested on the floor beside me. This suitcase had special significance. It was the latest in travel technology for the 1950s flying culture. Ultra-light, made of fine tan-colored Argentinean leather and canvas siding; it was quite different from the usual heavy, hard-sided Samsonite bags. It was very special; given to me by my Aunt Julia as a farewell and good fortune gift. It was also the symbol of a well-guarded secret revealing my transition from the inadequacy of adolescence to manhood.

I had fallen into a waking sleep when a strident voice announced the bus going to downtown Manhattan, which startled me awake. I picked up the suitcase, handed it to the driver to be placed in the luggage compartment, jumped on the bus, and sat in a window seat. The coolness of the vinyl upholstery absorbed some of my fatigue as I relaxed against it.

I thought tiredly of the long journey from home, with all the many stops for refueling in airport after airport. The end was now within reach; but I wondered how long it would be until I felt at home again.

As the bus started across the Brooklyn Bridge the city skyline came into view. It was impressive, but not frightening as I consider myself city-smart. I would live here for at least the next year. I had traded one multimillion populated city, Buenos Aires, for another much larger, New York City.

Leaving the bus at the 34th Street Station, I retrieved the suitcase containing all my life possessions and headed for the taxi stand. In those days, taxi drivers *did* speak English.

Unfortunately, I did not. Anticipating communication problems, I had written the address of the hospital on the back of a brochure from the bus terminal. It read:

Harlem Hospital
Lenox Avenue and 136th Street

I slid across the rear seat of the next free cab and handed the note to the driver who read it. He swiveled around to face me, sputtering a string of agitated words. Despite not understanding his words, by the few I could understand, coupled with the expression on the driver's face, I realized, in essence, the cabbie was telling me, "You don't want to go there."

"Yes," I nodded back vigorously in affirmation, "Yes, I do." I reached inside my jacket and pulled out the letter from the hospital that confirmed my appointment to a one-year internship at that address. I showed it to the driver. The cabbie read it in silence, shrugged his shoulders, and started the engine. Without another word he pulled out into the heavy traffic and headed uptown toward our destination. As we drove through wide avenues and narrow side streets, I congratulated myself at the success of my communication with the driver. I sat back enjoying the sights of the great city passing outside the windows. After a while we left Central Park, still heading north. I noticed that the aspect of the buildings began to change. Some apartment houses and storefronts were neglected and even dilapidated. Sidewalks were unkempt and spotted with trash. More and more black people walked the streets. Their clothing and general appearance was somehow different from the white people I had seen downtown. A feeling of uneasy apprehension washed over me once again. It was the onset of what I would term "my culture shock."

Growing up in Buenos Aires, a city of five million inhabitants, there were strong European cultural influences, mostly of Italian, Spanish, British and German ancestry. Blacks were practically unknown. In fact, there were few blacks in all of Argentina. I remembered only one black man, the driver of one of the ambulances at the hospital where I did my surgical residency. Occasionally, in downtown Buenos Aires, one would see a group of black people in shops or restaurants. Most often they were tourists from Brazil.

Months later, I would reflect on memories of history classes in primary school. We were taught with pride that the Negroes brought to Argentina by the Spanish slave trade had been liberated in 1813, shortly after Argentina gained its own independence. This was fifty years before Lincoln issued America's Emancipation Proclamation. We were taught that Argentina's liberated slaves eventually moved north to Brazil in search of warmer climate. I now realize sociologists might edit and correct those history lessons, as they were probably far from complete. But I did no such thinking riding uptown that afternoon, taking in all the general differences I noticed as their own kind of evidence. The people seemed different in more ways than just skin color.

Smoking a cigarette in the car, I began to wonder with some apprehension, *"where am I going?"* This was not the New York City I had envisioned. The possibility that the American film industry had sowed several misconceptions about the metropolis started to seep into my consciousness. Where were the monumental architectural skyscrapers, lush parks, and clean streets populated by happy-go-lucky, well-dressed white people?

"Well, here we are!" said the cabbie, dissolving my reverie.

We were parked in front of the main entrance. I got out and looked around in disbelief. The building was dirty and gray, a four-story limestone box with a peeling façade. The shabby crumbling frieze over the entrance door read, *Harlem Hospital.* I thought I must be reading the sign wrong. To the side of the steps leading to the entrance, a black woman in a worn overcoat and knitted winter hat was selling small bouquets of flowers out of an old, rusty baby carriage. It was a bizarre and surreal welcome.

I paid the fare, which left me with a grand total of twenty dollars and change; not much of a fortune. Luckily, the hospital contract included a stipend of sixty-eight dollars per month which would start immediately. I remembered how in Argentina that amount had seemed adequate. The driver set my suitcase on the curb, tossed a commiserating half-wave goodbye in my direction, and drove away.

Standing on the curb, suitcase by my side, I contemplated my new address. I had left my Buenos Aires medical career behind with little reservation, to try to further my knowledge and surgical skill, in the city my peers thought of as the mecca of scientific and medical learning. Even before I set foot in Harlem Hospital and the start of my training, I recognized my haste and began to regret the impetuousness of my decision. But it was too late! I had no choice but to swim.

The hospital Juan A. Hernandez in Buenos Aires, Argentina 1956.

The medical facility where I had practiced in Buenos Aires occupied an entire city block with twelve stories rising into the blue sky. The Juan A. Fernandez Hospital was a teaching hospital with almost every medical specialty available, located in an elegant, upper middle-class section of the city, surrounded by flowering gardens.

I knew instinctively not to stand too long at the curb or spend too long mulling over the decision I'd already made and acted upon. I picked up my suitcase with a twenty-five-year old's bravado and entered the building.

Working to maintain my composure, I went through the formalities of being admitted into the training program. I met with the hospital administrator and the chief of the medical staff, who briefly informed me of my duties and responsibilities. I understood little of what was said due to the language barrier. I was then guided by an office clerk to the living quarters; another disappointing surprise! My assigned room was in great need of refurbishing. In weeks to come, I would hear rumors that the old building had been condemned by the city inspector. It was easy to believe, although the hospital was in no hurry to make any remediation.

My roommate was a graduate of the University of Milan in Italy. At least we could communicate well enough in his native tongue.

Alfredo was a friendly man, in his early forties, who offered to introduce me to the rest of the interns and guide me through the routine of the job. He was half-way through his own internship year.

The next step was to locate my friend Enrique, which wasn't difficult. Enrique's room was just a few doors down the poorly lit corridor of the old building that housed all the interns.

A handwritten name appeared on a piece of white adhesive tape affixed to the door.

"ENRIQUE J. CASANELLO, MD"

He quickly answered my knock. His normally cheerful expression had been replaced by a dejected mask. We embraced with great emotion.

"How are things here?" were my first words.

After a long pause, Enrique replied in a low, discouraged voice, "Not what we expected; you'll find out." Unfortunately, my friend was right. In the weeks and months ahead, nothing would occur to contradict his bleak prophesy.

CHAPTER TWO

That night, as I lay in bed in the interns' quarters, in a room begging for a fresh coat of paint, I retraced my relationship with Enrique. We met during our military service. In 1950, in Argentina, when a young man approached his twentieth birthday, his name was automatically entered into the military lottery. Serving was compulsory, so the lottery just determined which branch would become home for the next calendar year or longer. Low numbers won a pair of army boots for the inductee, middle numbers sailed the navy's seas, and high numbers flew the skies as part of Argentina's burgeoning air force. I had received the letter on my twentieth birthday, November 14, 1950, along with the scheduled date for my physical exam, which I passed. I reported with other recruits to the Army Regiment of Buenos Aires the first week of January, 1951. From there, we were transferred to the Medical Unit of a Service Regiment on the outskirts of Buenos Aires. My goodbyes at home were somber; my family understood that they would not hear from me for the next three months of basic training.

◊ ◊ ◊

"Pack your gear and get on the bus outside!", I was ordered by the sergeant major.

The author in Argentinean Army 1951.

The author, second from the left, with fellow soldiers.

I joined a group of new recruits already on the bus. I felt an overwhelming feeling of despair and uncertainty, intensified when our questions were ignored by the sergeant in charge. They dropped us off at a nearby railroad station where we boarded a train headed north toward the province of Corrientes, a far away, rugged, subtropical region neighboring Brazil.

I had never traveled such a distance, nor been in a situation that removed me from making the decisions that structured my life. I had only been in the Medical Unit a few days, and now I was heading for the unknown. I realized that I had lost control of my life and was only a disposable pawn in the lower rank of the military. I was aware that I looked handsome in my uniform, even as I wondered if it might somewhat misidentify me. While the train labored across the vast landscape, lurching spastically along rough tracks, the dreaded feeling was replaced by edginess and fatigue. The weight of my uniform contributed to an unaccustomed lethargy. I felt adrift.

When the train finally arrived at the military installation near Paso de los Libres, a small city on the shores of the Uruguay River across from Brazil, I learned I had been assigned to an elite combat battalion. Struggling with the news, I reminded myself that service was for a finite period of time; that I was capable of performing the tasks assigned to me, and that more importantly, I had no choice. Yet the irony of the government's plan to use my life in combat was jarring. Only weeks before I had been deep into my third year of medical school, studying how to care for my fellow man. My confidence in government was as chafed as my body in its new uniform, and damp with the sweat of consternation and the heat of the region.

The next three months were a blur of enduring the boredom of repetition that develop agility; the constant physical challenges that fosters stamina, and the discipline that numbs one into mindless obedience. Constant stress taught me how to maintain the upper hand. I didn't want to know all the techniques they taught me concerning the many ways one human being can physically control, subdue, and even kill another. The emphasis was on hand-to-hand combat, martial arts as a system of self-defense, and sniper training. But the physical demands proved to be a Godsend, because by the end of each day my exhaustion was so profound that sleep showered my mind fresh. I hoped I would never need to rely on the split-second brutality learned there, yet the training taught me that I could function very well defensively if necessary.

Outwardly, I obeyed orders and excelled within my group. Inwardly, I focused on my own plans in order to stay emotionally intact, treating the present circumstance like the temporary government-sponsored interlude it was. I was grateful I had no compulsion to rebel against authority, because for those who did, life was difficult.

But by the end of basic training I knew it was time to speak up. "I've studied for a substantial amount of time to be of service to people in need of medical care," I told my commanding officer. "I've acquired skills that seem to be at odds with this program. Learning to kill people doesn't appear to fit. Isn't there somewhere I can serve that makes use of my medical training?"

To my great relief and surprise, I was soon reassigned back to my original medical outfit on the outskirts of Buenos Aires. At work in my new assignment, the mental chatter conjuring up shadows of imaginary enemies receded. I settled into working within a medical environment again. It was during this time that I met a fellow medical corpsman, Enrique Casanello, who would become a good friend and comrade-in-arms in an arena of real conflict that we would face together in the future.

While I was in school, and working at Fernandez Hospital, I had always loved the twenty-four-hour weekly placement in the Emergency Room (ER). Not knowing what would happen next was its best aspect. The noise of the ambulance announced the time had arrived to really practice medicine. I was no sensation-seeker, but as an eager student, the more chaotic the day the better the chance of developing much-needed skills.

Many patients required routine care, of course, but in the ER some would come for help, and *my* intervention, *my* knowledge, *my* skills, might determine the quality of the rest of that patient's life, or even whether that life would continue. The hyperfocus that channeled my energy enabled me to make split-second decisions. This was what I had feverishly studied for and where I knew I belonged. I hoped any major cases would come at times when I wasn't bone-weary, and less able to communicate and function effectively. The long rotations were designed so young doctors could learn to access untapped physical and mental reserves that were fundamental to their development. In the ER, mysteries of complicated illnesses and conditions were arrayed before me.

The Juan A. Fernandez hospital emergency surgical team;
Buenos Aries, Argentina. (1954)
The author is second from right of the front row.

I watched, learned, and performed well, mentored by experienced doctors. I thought about every aspect of my studies. I didn't think about the broad scope of medical services' delivery. Care was given to each patient with an equality of services I took for granted. At this point in my career I had no time to be interested in the protocols medical administrators designed and followed. I never thought of how the culture's political climate informed decisions of *how to treat* and *whom to treat*. The economics of medicine didn't interest me. I wanted only to practice caring for people, to be the one who intervened when their health and well-being were compromised. I loved interacting with people, but like my parents, professionally I saw myself as an individual contributor.

The months in the medical corps were just what I needed to erase the harshness of my military experiences up north. It felt like a return to sanity. Life made sense once more, and the friendship of Enrique added an element of balance to military service and life in general. I had someone I trusted and with whom I could share the work; we both understood the similarity of our personal goals.

We talked at length about every aspect of our lives. We were effortlessly compatible. As we shared our hopes and dreams, we dared to be ambitious and optimistic. Anything was possible. We would intern together somewhere. We believed restrictions were things that people placed on themselves through lack of imagination and laziness. We believed ourselves to be cultivators of confidence, not braggadocios.

Without knowing, Enrique and I had been students at the same medical school. We marveled that we hadn't met each other before our military service. I completed my military duty in March of 1952, and like Enrique, still had educational requirements to complete. Medical school was a six-year program; however, I stepped in and out of my continuum for the interruption of military service was facilitated with ease.

We didn't spend all of our time studying or with patients. We wanted to have fun, and also make money for personal expenses.

One lucky contact made the necessity of jobs more interesting, enjoyable, and lucrative than our previous employment. A neighbor, and friend of my family named Roberto, was the maitre d' of the nightclub *Sans-souci* a high class *boite de nuit* in downtown Buenos Aires. City ordinances prohibited women without escorts from entering establishments alone to discourage prostitution. Thanks to Roberto, my friend and I were hired as "taxi boys" to circumvent this law. All that was required of a taxi boy was to accompany one "lady" at a time from a discrete pick up spot, out of sight and a short distance from the club, along the street and into the establishment. The woman would then slip me the equivalent of about five dollars for five minutes' work and I would saunter back to retrieve the next customer needing squiring to the club. This scenario was repeated as often as necessary to keep the business running. The monetary benefits were substantial. Perhaps, more important was the experience gained by navigating in a quasi-legal underground cultural environment.

We were careful not to discuss the nature of our new employment at home since our parents would disapprove. The job was almost devoid of the danger and physical exertion of my former work as a messenger, pedaling documents throughout the financial district in heavy city traffic, though I may have become a little less fit as time went by.

Exactly what fantasies we both enjoyed as we escorted the ladies to work we kept to ourselves, though exposure to this interesting nightlife may have spawned the idea of how brilliant it would be to try to intern in Paris. Our familial histories were entwined with Europe's, both families immigrating only two generations earlier. Why not experience the exotic flavor of *The City of Light,* and at the same time further our education? Spanish and French were both Romance languages. We figured that we should be able to manage the new one with ease.

Unfortunately, the French didn't have the welcome mat out. French hospitals accepted only students who had matriculated at French schools. With our Argentinean education, we didn't qualify. We were disappointed with our abortive inquiries, but not disheartened, and decided to check out the Lincoln Library, a small cultural annex of the U.S. Embassy in downtown Buenos Aires. It offered books in English, periodicals, and American magazines. The library subscribed to JAMA, *the Journal of the American Medical Association*, and the October/November issue featured internship programs offered by hospitals in the United States.

It listed the names and addresses of specific institutions and the requirements for admission to each program state-by-state. Some requirements, such as U.S. citizenship, graduation from an American medical school or medical licensure in a particular state, disqualified us from applying.

With some language help from the librarian, we managed to discover approximately thirty hospitals scattered across the country for which we had the appropriate credentials. Most commonly, these programs commenced on July first of each year. Applications were reviewed and evaluated in mid-January.

The same helpful librarian and a volunteer assistant worked with us to compose an application template. With this in hand we now only needed to type separate letters for each submission, a daunting task accomplished with the aid of my sister Nora, a teacher with adequate typing skills and the requisite cheerfulness.

With great effort we completed the project and mailed the letters to the hospitals. And then, all we could do was wait.

To our pleasure we both received offers before the end of November from Harlem Hospital, a New York City facility located in Upper Manhattan. Each offer included a contract for a one-year rotating internship, a stipend of $68.00 per month, free room and board, free uniforms, and laundry services. It wasn't a fortune, but for two young men from Buenos Aires in 1955, it seemed like a livable wage and a stellar opportunity.

Enrique's contract listed a starting date of January 15, 1956. Mine "on or about" February 16. We were drunk with delight. We would live in New York City! Our dreams were gaining momentum and definition, and we didn't even have to wait until the official registration date of July first.

The possibilities of our new lives elated us. Without delay, we accepted our respective offers. Our only interest in further investigation was limited to how to get there, to the next phase of our charmed lives.

"Haste makes waste" is a universal adage whose wisdom is often ignored by the young, especially when bedazzled. We limited our research to obtaining visas and finding the quickest way to apply and receive entrance. "Student Visa" seemed to aptly describe our situation, and the process was so much quicker than applying for a "Permanent Visa." So, we chose the former.

The word "permanent" threw us off simply because we had no intention of staying in the States. Why go through a more involved process to obtain something we didn't need in the first place? We would be in America two or three years at most, depending on our luck in generating residency placements. Returning home was our goal. Smart enough to be successful students, engaged and ambitious enough to breeze through our daily lives, we lacked the maturity to ask ourselves under what circumstances it might be a good idea to provide for more than our basic needs.

During the second week of January, I accompanied Enrique to the airport and bid him goodbye. "I'll see you shortly in New York!" I said with a foolish grin.

"Integrate into the American way of life," has long been the advice given to those arriving on these shores. Unfortunately, life as an intern and the social environment at Harlem Hospital were not conducive to social adaptation. I soon discovered that I had to put in long hours doing hardly more than orderly's work, routine chores that were not done by doctors in my country. As interns at the hospital, we learned nothing in the medical field that we didn't already know. We were the hospital's answer to a severe labor shortage: exploit foreign students by capitalizing on American medicine's international reputation. Compounding that frustration was our language inadequacy which created obstacles to relating to colleagues, save for those few who spoke Spanish or Italian.

Communicating with the nursing staff and hospital workers was accomplished with few words and much gesturing. Twice-a-week English classes were offered to foreign trainees, but they dealt mainly with technical medical terminology and minimally with conversational English or vocabulary. It was hardly enough to overcome the stress of daily interactions. Not being able to verbalize your thoughts was interpreted as a lack of competence in the performance of duties. We resented the lack of opportunity to practice medicine, to improve our skills, and to be treated as a valued member of the medical community in which we labored.

I knew that improving my language skills had to be a major priority. In the course of daily work assignments, I met a black nurse of Hispanic descent who spoke Spanish quite fluently. She shared information about an adult education program at a local high school and explained how to register.

I passed that information on to Enrique and on one of our days off we visited the school and enrolled in the *Basic English* course offered three evenings a week. Fortunately, these programs were funded by the city's Department of Education at no cost to participants. We attended as often as our work schedules allowed. I was very enthusiastic about learning conversational English because it's difficult to help someone you can hardly talk to, and because many staff doctors treated foreign interns with little respect. I recognized the dismissive behavior by their tone and body language but had no way to refute them without language proficiency. It would be years before the global culture would shrink enough for hospitals to attempt to provide language services, even in America's largest cities.

Attending night school gave me the opportunity not only to improve my ability to communicate, but to meet other more seasoned newcomers to the States. Everyone was friendly and congenial, bonded into community by being strangers in a new land.

I soon developed a close relationship with a man named Luis and his girlfriend Amanda, both from Guatemala. They lived in nearby Spanish Harlem and worked in a travel agency catering to the Hispanic population in the area. Amanda had been a teacher and Luis had a degree in mechanical engineering. We became good friends, and through them, I began to learn there was a vibrant society outside the boundaries of the marginalized black neighborhood where the hospital was situated.

The limitations of the internship's program disappointed and frustrated me. I was there to learn and couldn't quite believe so little was done to honor the implied provisions of the contract Harlem Hospital had offered and I had signed. I was always looking for the opportunity to demonstrate my surgical capabilities.

After completing three months in the medical service, I was assigned to the *Surgical Unit* as part of the rotating program. This assignment was very hard to endure. My initial hopefulness gradually changed to anger as I realized my duties were restricted to menial nursing work such as cleaning and changing surgical dressings after procedures were performed by others. No consideration was given to the fact that I had previous surgical training in my country, and I was experienced in performing appendectomies, hernia repairs, and other abdominal procedures.

Residents looked down, not only on me, but on the other three interns in the unit. Long work hours included frequent nights and weekends on call. When discussing my future plans with some friendly surgical residents and a few attending surgeons, I discovered that openings to surgical programs were mostly limited to graduates from American medical schools and to a very few foreign graduates with connections. There was no comfort in learning that nepotism in the surgical community was rampant.

My next assignment was the *Emergency Service*, considered the best rotation in the program. Interns worked shifts of 8 hours, seven days a week with no extra duties, and had the opportunity to deal with challenging medical and surgical cases, including many traumatic injuries. I felt at home within this busy and demanding structure. I applied my skills and learned from challenging new experiences.

The work schedule consisted of seven days of 8-hour shifts; one week from 8 a.m. to 4 p.m.; followed by a 4 p.m. to midnight week; and the next week from midnight to 8 a.m. This rotation continued for two months with no days off.

During one Saturday night shift, a man in his thirties was brought to the ER after sustaining a 12-inch laceration to his left arm as a result of a knife fight. The slash ran from his shoulder almost to his elbow. The case was assigned to me.

After ruling out any injury to the nerves and underlying blood vessels, I carefully sutured the gaping wound. I was so focused that I didn't notice one of the surgeons from the Surgical Unit looking over my shoulder and observing my work. When I completed the task, the doctor spoke.

"What's your name, doctor?"

Startled, I quickly replied, "DeNapoli doctor, Jorge DeNapoli. I'm one of the interns." "I'm Doctor James Walker, and I was observing your technique. Have you had any previous surgical training?"

"Yes, Dr. Walker, I practiced surgery for two years before coming to the States." "Good. Could I talk with you in the office when you've finished with the case?" "I'll be glad to, doctor."

When we met in the office at the nurse's station, we shook hands. "It's nice to meet you, Dr. DeNapoli."

"Glad to meet you, Dr. Walker."

These few words represented the only respectful exchange I had had to date with a professional on staff. Dr. Walker went on to say he'd been observing my performance in the ER and was impressed by my suturing ability. "Have you rotated in surgery?"

"Yes, Doctor."

"I don't seem to recall your name."

"I rotated in surgery, but never had the opportunity to assist in the OR," I said cautiously. "Have you considered a surgical residency here at the hospital? I would like you to be one of my assistants when I operate. I will talk with the chairman of the department. See me in my office on Tuesday."

"Thank you, Doctor. I'll be there."

I couldn't contain my excitement and couldn't wait to share the good news with Enrique. When I was finally off duty, I ran to his room, finding him still awake and reading a medical journal. I blurted out the story of my encounter with Dr. Walker. Enrique congratulated me, but asked incredulously, "Do you really think he'd offer you a residency here?" His question burst my bubble.

"Doctor Walker seemed quite sincere," I murmured defensively.

"What about that letter from the Doctor at Presbyterian Hospital?" Enrique asked. I hadn't thought of that correspondence in a long while. We reflectively recalled the events leading up to the writing of it; our thoughts winging poignantly back to another time in a cleaner, faraway place.

One day, while Enrique and I were assigned to the Emergency Room at the Fernandez Hospital in Buenos Aires, a young American tourist in her early twenties was brought in with multiple facial injuries. She had been involved in an automobile accident and her head had struck the windshield of the car. A blood-stained towel was wrapped around her head and face. Examination by one of the ER doctors found multiple deep lacerations of the scalp, forehead, and both maxillary areas. X-rays revealed no fractures of the facial bones. She was alert but in severe pain. These were her only injuries. She was sedated and another intern had started her on an IV solution of fluids.

I happened to be on call that day. My colleagues in the ER knew I was part of the surgical team and delved into special suturing techniques involving facial and other visible lacerations. I was called to take charge. I meticulously examined the scalp and facial injuries. I then spent almost three hours carefully using intradermal sutures to close her lacerations, practicing the latest techniques I had discovered in my studies. When finished, I proudly reassessed the work done. The facial area was still covered with bruises and excoriations, but the lacerations showed only as fine lines on her attractive young face.

Hours later, a relative and several friends took the young woman back to the hotel where they were staying. The patient was scheduled to return in two days for a follow-up visit to re-evaluate her injuries, but she failed to reappear.

I had almost forgotten about this particular incident, when months later a letter arrived at the hospital, addressed to my name, from a Dr. Bradford Peterson, a plastic surgeon practicing at the Columbia-Presbyterian Hospital in New York City. Dr. Peterson praised my excellent surgical repairs. The young woman had consulted him for further treatment of her injuries. "The lacerations were hardly visible and only minor reconstruction was needed." I flushed with great pride. The letter added that, if at any time, I were visiting New York City, I should call on him. "It will be a pleasure to meet you personally," it concluded. I had proudly shared the contents of the doctor's letter with my associates and eventually filed it with other significant documents.

Perhaps Enrique was right. Had I brought the letter with me to America?

I started my 4 p.m. to midnight workweek anticipating Tuesday's meeting with Dr. Walker. By Tuesday morning I had over-thought all the possibilities. I was a jumble of conflicting feelings. I wanted the opportunity to use my surgical skills but didn't want to extend my stay at Harlem Hospital. But sometimes fate steps in to make decisions for us. My dilemma was solved quickly after our conversation. I arrived at the doctor's small, plain office on the surgical floor. After a few formalities, Dr. Walker reported, "I talked with the department chief, but he disapproved of any such arrangement. The chief feels it will be contrary to hospital protocols and disruptive to the internship and residency program. I'm sorry. Maybe I can talk with him again later to see if he'll change his position."

*The author at the main entrance to Harlem Hospital, New York City.
(circa 1956)*

Enrique, and a friend with the author at Harlem Hospital. (1956)

I thanked him for his efforts and returned to my quarters, both disappointed and relieved that I didn't have to commit myself to a longer stay. Enrique had been right in warning me to guard against being too optimistic.

That evening, when Enrique's shift in pediatrics had finished for the day, he spoke with me about the news and its implications.

"Consider yourself lucky," said Enrique. "You don't need to stay here longer than our contract. Don't waste your time with the people here. Go and see Dr. Peterson at the Presbyterian."

We talked for quite a while. Enrique repeatedly encouraging me to follow the offer in Dr. Peterson's letter. "You're right," I finally agreed. "That's my best option."

Since I didn't start work until 4 p.m. I had time to pursue the next step. I searched the voluminous city telephone directory for Dr. Peterson's number before realizing the letter from him, on office stationery, had all the information I would need. I sprinted back to look for the letter, which turned out to be safely guarded in the file I kept locked in the suitcase under my bed. Clutching it like a life preserver, I rushed to the telephone booth in the intern's lounge.

I made the call and was encouraged by the friendly voice of the department secretary. Introducing myself, I requested an appointment. "Dr. Peterson is in surgery and has a full schedule next week. I could give you an appointment on Friday after the doctor's surgical rounds. Would 11 a.m. be all right?"

"That will be fine. I'll be there Friday at 11," I responded quickly, "Thank you."

As I hung up, my mind leaped toward several wonderful possibilities, but I checked *myself* quickly. I had been disillusioned enough since my arrival. I allowed myself one all- inclusive indulgence. *Maybe*, I mused *my luck is about to change.*

I woke early Friday after a night spent planning and rehearsing. It was critical that I use my best English. I didn't want to have to hunt for a single word in the doctor's presence. This man had already shown himself to be a gracious professional, but I wasn't sure how far his courtesy would extend. I ate breakfast in the dining hall while simultaneously scribbling phrases on a piece of paper. *Would I be able to speak them fluently when the time came?*

"What are you writing?" Enrique asked as he joined me at the table.

"Things I want to discuss with Dr. Peterson," was my reply. "I don't want him to think I have problems communicating."

"Good Luck!" Enrique said sarcastically; then edited his words and attitude. "Seriously, good luck."

I arrived at the impressive building of the Columbia-Presbyterian Hospital on the west side of Upper Manhattan, walked to the front desk, and asked for directions to the Surgical Department. I was directed to the elevators that accessed the surgical floor. When the doors opened and I stepped off, I looked like a lad from the country, head swiveling from side-to-side admiring the bright, sterile atmosphere. It was everything I had anticipated a hospital in New York City to be, quite a contrast to Harlem.

I introduced myself at the reception desk. "I'm Dr. Jorge DeNapoli."

The small name card on the secretary's desk read, "Karen Mulcahy."

"Dr. Peterson is finishing his rounds. He'll be with you shortly. Please take a seat," she smiled, motioning to a well-appointed waiting area. "May I offer you a cup of coffee, Doctor?"

"No thank you, Karen," I replied, trying to establish a more personal contact by using her first name. I knew from experience that secretaries are the influential gatekeepers to their bosses.

I sat on a comfortable stuffed chair facing the entrance to the surgical unit. Through the glass inserts in the doors, I could see crisp hospital-dressed nurses and white coated doctors moving about busily. I felt benched on the sidelines. This was my playing field. I felt a not unpleasant anxiety building in anticipation of the meeting. Hopeful anticipation threatened to derail my concentration. The excitement of possibilities had always driven me to imagine, believe, and project into my future. The only time it had failed me was in saying, 'Yes' too quickly to the Harlem Hospital internship. Now that I understood this creative energy could derail my progress, I made every attempt to restrain it.

Dr. Peterson brushed both doors aside as he strode into the waiting area. He was a tall, athletic-looking man with slightly graying hair and dark-rimmed glasses. Smiling, he approached me.

"Dr. DeNapoli, welcome to New York and to my workplace." He offered his hand.

Obviously his secretary had informed him of my arrival. I stood up, shook hands and mumbled an intimidated, "Thank you, nice to meet you, Doctor."

"Let's go to my office where we can talk, away from this frenzy," the doctor said, turning to move down the wide hall. I followed the furling flaps of his white coat as it glided smoothly into a large office overlooking the Hudson River. A multitude of letters, medical reports and patient files were spread across a wide mahogany desk. A graceful sculpture soared in swirled steel shapes, evoking the dynamics of dueling sails plying the river below. Fine art graced the walls along with extravagantly framed diplomas.

Dr. Peterson sat behind his desk and motioned for me to sit. Positioned opposite this self- assured professional in his high-back leather chair, I couldn't help to view him as a judge – or executioner.

Dr. Peterson asked a number of questions; first about my travel to the States, then about my medical education and my surgical experience, and recent work at Harlem Hospital. He revisited the case of the young woman with facial injuries, and again congratulated me on my efficient surgical skills. Finally he asked me to comment about my adaptation to American life and my command of the language. I pounced on the chance to share my goal of pursuing more specialized surgical training, hoping my passion for the field and the desire to excel in practicing could be conveyed in my broken English. I concluded, "If there was any way, Dr. Peterson that you could help…"

Dr. Peterson paused reflectively. His expression indicated he was about to say something unpleasant. His tone was detached.

"Dr. DeNapoli, you're speaking of a difficult field to enter. The surgical community is a very exclusive club. The requirements are set quite high. Preference is given to American graduates who have completed their internships at prestigious hospitals. Harlem Hospital hardly meets that criterion. You're in a position to know that as well as anyone, and, to be frank, your English needs much improvement. I'm sorry to tell you all this, but I'm trying to be clear that you have a tremendously difficult, if not impossible, road ahead of you. I can't paint a brighter picture."

So there it was. I had been hanging on each word, because I had abrogated my future to this great and imposing man. I had not expected such calculated words delivered with cool condescension. I managed to mention the evening classes at the high school, trying to make the case that I was doing everything I could to better learn the language, not just for the doctor's benefit but for my own self-respect. This was the attitude that formed my psyche, the bedrock on which I had anchored the construction of my future life.

"I'll consult with the chairman and see how we might be able to help you. I'll get in touch with you at your hospital," said Dr. Peterson, terminating the interview.

I managed to thank him and left, phrases swirling in my ears, my natural enthusiasm deflated by the harsh sentence this man, representing everything I admired, had pronounced. The usual, "I'll talk to the Chief," sent away, again – nothing but excuses. I heard nothing further from the gracious Dr. Peterson.

Riding the subway back to Harlem, I had difficulty containing my anger. I had never seen myself as a victim and didn't now. Plans were what *I* made and carried out. *I* created my own life, it did not just happen to me. But, since our mistake of taking the internship at Harlem Hospital, based on youthful joy rather than careful analysis, I felt as if the work of my hands amounted to nothing more than good intentions. I had worked conscientiously yet gained nothing. My assurance of being on the right path I chose and strode along had somehow become transformed into a scene where I watched myself plod down a dreary street, without noticing that it was marked *DOA,* meaning Dead On Arrival in this culture. Why? It was beyond my understanding. Why did these men have the power to deny access to someone capable, motivated, and energetic? I had no answers or insights. I felt only rage.

Making a satisfactory social adjustment was another matter. Gradually, I was learning the language. Through my new friends, Luis and Amanda, and classmates in the evening courses at the high school, I expanded my social life, meeting a number of men and women my age. The drawback was that all of these acquaintances were Latin American.

Weekend nights when not on duty, Enrique and I attended dancing events planned by Spanish-speaking organizations from a variety of Latin America countries. At the very first dance we attended, I was denied entrance. "Anglos are not allowed," the gate keeper barked.

Obviously, he had been misled by my appearance. Since I was a tall, slender young man with blond hair and blue eyes, I had frequently been mistaken as German, Austrian or Swedish. In perfect Spanish, with an Argentinian accent, I promptly convinced the doorman of my nationality.

At one of the dances, I met a young native of Colombia who worked as a nurse at St. Vincent's Hospital in mid-town Manhattan. We developed a close relationship, and after dating for about two months, she invited me to have dinner with her and her parents at their home in Jackson Heights, Queens. A huge red flag went up, but I was not about to miss a free home cooked meal. I was guided by my stomach more than by my heart or mind.

A medical doctor having to go hungry in America was totally inconceivable and unexplained by American standards, but a number of times that is exactly what Enrique and I experienced: real hunger. Sometimes, because of having to work overtime, we missed dinner, since the dining hall closed at 8 pm. On those occasions we put together all our small change, enough to buy a barbecued chicken or pulled pork sandwich from the small, unsanitary shop across from the hospital, which we shared. We might splurge and have a beer or two at a nearby bar right after pay day. Otherwise, our financial situation demanded frugality. Sometimes we were completely broke. We eventually befriended two fellow countrymen, owners of a small luncheonette located on Amsterdam Ave., catering mostly to Hispanics.

Many weekend nights, the two of us worked behind the counter, not just to help our friends but to secure a free meal. It is amazing how a full stomach could mitigate the feelings of anger and frustration over an inconceivable situation.

The dinner in Queens was excellent with dessert and wine. Riding the bus back to my room, I experienced the uncharacteristic feeling of a full stomach paired with the nagging certainty that I needed to cool the relationship. I was neither ready, nor willing, to enter any formal commitment. The relationship that had climaxed on the occasion of that fine evening eventually faded away.

During the first six months of my arrival, I met girls from Mexico, Costa Rica, Colombia, Puerto Rico and other Spanish speaking countries, but no actual native-born Americans. In jest, one of the Hispanic interns used to say, "When I arrived in this country, I was told that in order to learn English, I had to date American girls. I didn't learn much English, but I surely had a lot of fun." Truthfully, there had been no chance for me to meet any American girls.

Among the young medical group at the hospital, sex was a frequent topic of conversation. Usually a group of eight to ten Spanish-speaking white interns and residents sat together at a large table in the dining hall; not necessarily self-segregated. These doctors would freely discuss sexual relations they had had or were having with Negro nurses or administrative personnel. I had no such experiences, until one night while covering the Emergency Pediatrics Service, I met Sylvia, a twenty-two year old nurse's aide. During those years in America, darker Negroes used the term *high yellow* to describe Sylvia's lighter coloring. It was not meant to be complimentary. I lumped the term with a number of racial and ethnic slurs I had come to understand the meaning of, within the context of how black Americans treated one another. The complexity of the social environment was not

34

structured on individual worth as human beings but on characteristics of ethnicity or appearances. This harsh treatment of minorities tarnished my notion of America and, for a time, tainted my acceptance of what was, at the time, a highly segregated minority group still referred to as Negroes. However, I didn't have the time to think about such cultural expressions until I was more fluent in the language and the American way of life and could step over and through the limitations of its boundaries.

Enrique had already rotated through pediatrics and had mentioned Sylvia as someone who was *very friendly* to white interns. She was an attractive young woman who did little to conceal her willingness to start a relationship.

In my best possible English, I invited her to meet the following day in a café near the hospital. She was from North Carolina and had come to New York alone the year before. She lived in a one-bedroom apartment a few blocks away and mentioned that she felt uncomfortable meeting a white guy in a public place, a plausible thought in the late fifties. Instead, she invited me invited me to her apartment. She wrote the address on a scrap of paper and handed it to me with a seductive smile What followed was a torrid affair that lasted until I left the hospital months later.

Sylvia did a great deal for me. My relationship with her was a significant factor in improving my conversational skills. She encouraged me to talk with her, correcting my pronunciation and teaching me American idiomatic expressions. To this day, a hint of North Carolinian drawl wafts through my spoken English.

Another source of companionship came from Sunday afternoon dances at the Wagner Hall in Yorktown, the German section of New York City. These were attended by young adult Germans and other European immigrants, many of whom were recent arrivals. Broken English was the common language, with varying expression, making communicating that much more interesting. One day, Enrique and I discussed our mutual success with blue-eyed blondes.

Enrique, tall, handsome, and dark-haired seemingly had a slight edge, with characteristics sought out by the young European girls. Our contrasting looks made us a good team.

On many occasions, we wandered around nightclubs and bars located on Seventh Avenue. We discovered that cheap draft beer could be had in the seedy dives located in the basements of dilapidated buildings where live music thrived. Listening gave us real pleasure, and we had the good fortune of hearing many budding performers playing *progressive jazz*, the furor of the times. Occasionally we came across some very well-known artists. Some places banned *white folks*. We never felt threatened, but we were always vigilant with our senses heightened for possible danger.

From day one, ER rotation instructions included a firm warning of never to dismiss a chest or abdominal puncture wound as a minor injury, as it could prove to be the result of an ice pick thrust, the preferred defensive weapon of the female population. What looked like a shallow cut was often a deep penetrating wound. A woman would typically carry one in her pocketbook at all times. Sylvia had shown me hers with its six-inch steel shaft.

Because Enrique and I, as well as other interns and residents, were easily identified as *doctors from the hospital*, we were readily accepted into the often violent neighborhoods of Harlem. We seemed to be exempt from trouble. In fact, many times someone would approach with an offer to buy us a drink, because they, or a relative, had been treated by one of us in the ER or another of the hospital's wards. There must have been an awareness that we were also discriminated against, within a society that neither could integrate completely. Either that or the universal language of caring superseded other messages the language of color and culture conveyed.

Enrique, coincidentally, or by design, always dated girls with status of some sort. One was a nurse, the daughter of the Chief of Gynecology. Because she or her family couldn't attend, she'd given Enrique two tickets to the famous Apollo Theater on 125th Street. As a result, we had the chance to see an unforgettable performance from Ella Fitzgerald, the only whites in a sea of black faces that memorable night. On other Friday and Saturday evenings we enjoyed walking around Times Square. Sometimes we went to a movie on 42nd Street, and preferred the mezzanine seats where smoking was allowed.

In the days following the meeting with Dr. Peterson, I was in a nasty mood. Clearly I had to find and implement an alternative plan, though time stalled and we accomplished little in the next few months, while I grieved. Meanwhile, our internships crawled too slowly toward their end.

CHAPTER THREE

Early on what should have been an ordinary day, everything changed once again. Enrique and I learned that Argentinean medical colleagues intended to buy a well-known, multidisciplinary private clinic in Palermo, an upscale neighborhood in the northern section of Buenos Aires. The *Clinica Bazterrica*, with in-patient facilities for approximately thirty patients, had an excellent reputation within the medical community. The organizing group was inviting us to become participants, with me as part of the surgical team and Enrique managing the gynecology department. The clinic was selling for $700,000 American dollars. Each member of the team could buy in with a tenth of the purchase price. It was great news for Enrique, but not for me. Enrique came from a moderately well-to-do family and could borrow the required amount from his parents. My family was positioned squarely in the lower middle class and could not help financially. In America, I may have been able to secure a long-term loan by using my potential earning power and an additional life insurance policy as collateral. In Argentina, no such possibility existed.

I was born in San Antonio Oeste, Territory of Rio Negro, a modest railroad outpost that formed a hub that opened the gateway to the arid steppe-like plains of Patagonia, bare of vegetation but rich in underground oil reserves. The bright stars of the Southern Cross welcomed me, smiling down on the birth that increased the population of the little hamlet to almost eight hundred. The frigid waters of the South Atlantic washed those Argentine shores.

San Antonio Oeste had once been a required stop for *The End of the World Train,* which carried hardened and dangerous convicts to the infamous, high security penal colony in Ushuaia, Tierra del Fuego. This southernmost place inhabited year-round was separated from Antarctica by less than fifty miles of icy waves. Surely, my birthplace was an apt spot for a self-reliant child to begin life. Some would say this setting alone had bonded the luck of being born under the Southern Cross to my wandering spirit.

The majority of people living there worked for the government-owned railroad company, either in the small train station or the large warehouse, well-stocked with mechanical parts supporting oil production and the railroad's maintenance. My father worked as a clerk in the company's managing department, arriving three years earlier from the central office in Buenos Aires on a voluntary four-year program. He had been enticed to this remote location by the promise of a better position upon its completion. Seven years and three children later, the family was finally transferred back to the main office in Buenos Aires, the city where I grew up and considered my home.

My family was close-knit and hardworking. My parents had completed only the grammar school curriculum, but both were avid readers. A frequent topic of conversation at the dinner table was the importance of education. They constantly encouraged us; a large bookcase full of all sorts of reading material was pivotal to our home and our lives.

I looked up to my older brother Omar, and I was aware that I, too, had a responsibility to be worthy of being looked up to by my younger sister, Nora. All of us felt loved and supported, but responsible for our own success. We viewed our good fortune as confirmation that the paths we traveled were a proper reflection of correct assumptions.

Omar had graduated with a degree in business and accounting, and was employed in the financial department of a large maritime shipping company. Since his teen years, literature had been important to him, and later, as a hobby, he had taken courses in creative writing. He eventually became a prolific and successful author while still retaining his accounting job. He became well-known in local literary circles, receiving many accolades for his published collections of short stories.

Nora chose education, earning a master's degree, qualifying her for a secondary school teaching position in a suburb of Buenos Aires. During our years of study, each of us had worked in various part-time jobs to help defray our educational expenses.

I had always been comfortable with my history and had shared the particulars of my family, though a strong sense of privacy prevented me from discussing the emotional dynamics of our stories. I hadn't equivocated stories I shared with Enrique along the way, but it had taken until now for me to comprehend how a lack of financial privilege limits one's possibilities.

Once Enrique realized how difficult it had been for me to be completely open during this personal crisis, I could talk without pretense to him again.

Enrique reacted to the offer to buy into the Clinica Bazterrica with the joy of a man released from hopeless captivity. Each day had been a battle against the despair of our compromised dignity and self-recriminations. Now he raced through the tunnel of his grief toward a rapidly intensifying light. His significant struggles with the depression caused by our substandard internship evaporated the way thin morning haze burns off at dawn under bright sunshine. Enrique assumed it was my liberation, too. After all, we had been in this together from the start.

As comrades-in-arms, we had worn our voices hoarse discussing how to resolve the farce of our internship. Enrique had wanted to bolt for home from the first, but I had been adamant that the best way out was finishing our internship. I thought leaving would have marked us with a stigma of failure that would prove impossible to dispel. Now, Enrique was going to be free, while I was still trapped, lacking even the money for the plane fare home.

Enrique's lifeline miraculously appeared before I had recovered from the interview with Dr. Peterson, knocking me back off the meager balance I'd been able to achieve. One sentence looped through my mind incessantly: *There must be something I can do.* But what that something might be I couldn't will into being. I didn't begrudge Enrique his redemption. Our friendship was real. I was acutely aware of Enrique's daily struggle with self-directed blame for blindly accepting the internship offer.

The shame of being part of this dishonest practice of manipulating foreign doctors for the rest of their lives was real. We certainly had been *had,* and we were too smart to have let it happen. It wasn't as personal a failing for me, simply because I was more practical. I could only repeat that I had to find a way out. Diminishing Enrique's joyous good fortune was unthinkable.

Unsure for the first time in my life, I wondered how I could do without my friend's support. I thought of the sadness of being isolated while still in this excruciating pain. Every time that looped sentence played in my mind, my sense of panic was reactivated. Perhaps there *was* no way out. Perhaps I would have to let go and get sucked down into the new image of myself that threatened to engulf my existence. There was little respite from this fear.

Whenever we were together, our discussions revolved around topics concerning the clinic. We spent our free time anticipating every aspect of the transaction. Timing concerned Enrique. The investment firm wished to finalize the sale by the first week in December. If we were going to participate, we would have to break our contracts. There was no question that this was a sacrifice we would be only too happy to make.

At first, denial gave me some relief by offering the pretense of escape with my friend. Soon, I could no longer indulge in it without being cognizant I was simply too embarrassed to admit there was no way I could finance a getaway. The deceit I felt by not leveling with Enrique tormented me. I eventually recognized that the charade was nothing more than a coping mechanism and was grossly unfair to my colleague, and I finally built up enough courage to set the record straight.

"Enrique, I feel badly about waiting to tell you, but at the present time it's impossible for me to put together $70,000 dollars. I would obviously like to be part of the team," I acknowledged, "but not now. Maybe later on if there's still an opening I could join you guys." I said apologetically, indulging in one last dodge, fully aware they were just words.

At first, Enrique was stunned. We had talked at such length, projecting each other into the future. We'd made so many plans about the clinic, savoring such deliciously anticipated success. I watched while Enrique gradually absorbed my confession. I could see the thought dawn on him that it should never have been such news to him. We had been friends for years, always confiding to each other the true aspects of our lives.

"Accept the offer and go. This is the opportunity of a lifetime. I'll finish my year here, and when I get back home, the Clinica can hire me as a consultant," I offered as a wry joke. The reality that I *would* be left behind was not on the table. Without another word, we hugged. "I'm so sorry, Jorge," murmured Enrique, and left the room.

At the end of October Enrique submitted his two weeks' notice of resignation. His parents booked a return flight for him, leaving for Argentina a few days later. He had already sent his letter of acceptance to the investment firm.

I also wrote to the firm declining their offer, mentioning my intention to pursue surgical training in the US, and that I might consider joining them later if such an opening still existed.

Months before, I had met a fellow countryman, Fernando Astigueta, who was a psychiatric resident-in-training at Bellevue Hospital in New York City. We had met socially on a number of occasions and from our conversations, I learned that state psychiatry hospitals in other parts of the country were seeking foreign physicians to fill positions, offering well-paying salaries and requiring minimal psychiatric experience.

During many sleepless nights trying to generate ways to rescue my future, I considered every possibility I could unearth. After Enrique left, I missed him and our exchange of ideas, as well as his sincere advice. I still had friends on the medical staff, but not anyone close enough to have an open dialog with about my troubling preoccupations. Gradually, though, the shadowy outline of a plan had begun to take shape.

I visited Fernando and asked him about specific offers of psychiatric positions. Together we went to Bellevue's library and consulted the classified ads in the *Journal of Psychiatric Medicine*. We found that state hospitals in Massachusetts offered tempting salaries to attract staff psychiatrists. The requirements for these positions were rather liberal: graduation from a qualified medical school, a temporary license to practice medicine in Massachusetts, participation in a psychiatric review program, and a permanent visa to reside in the United States. Vacancies were available in several hospitals, but none in Boston. The nearest was Gardner State Hospital in Gardner, a city approximately an hour west of Boston. I collected all the necessary information. On my way back to Harlem Hospital I thought long and hard about how to avoid making the previous mistake when applying for my internship. I wanted no surprises this time! I would do my homework and carefully investigate all aspects of my plan.

I made a mental assessment of my situation and alternative short-term solutions. After some serious thinking I decided the best option was to return home. But, I was broke. I needed to make some money to pay for air fare and to rent an apartment in Buenos Aires. Going back to live with my parents was not an option. Also, opening even a small surgical practice would require some investment. I knew I would do well. I had friends and good connections within the medical community.

In my free time I persistently worked on my plan. I had developed a friendship with a surgical resident from the Philippines who spoke English and Spanish fluently. Augusto Felix had been born in Manila, the son of missionaries from Spain. I approached him for help in composing a letter to the Board of

Registration in Medicine, in Boston, inquiring if the University of Buenos Aires was on the list of qualified medical schools, and requesting an application for a temporary medical license in Massachusetts.

Within days their reply confirmed that the University of Buenos Aires was a qualified school, and an application form for temporary licensure was enclosed.

So far, so good, I rejoiced.

Next, I drafted a letter to Gardner State Hospital applying for the open position. Augusto corrected the letter to some extent, but not to the point of making it look too perfect as I didn't want them to think that it had been written by someone else. It stated that I would not be available to accept the position immediately as I needed time to obtain the temporary license and a permanent visa.

The reply from the hospital offered a position as a staff psychiatrist with a monthly salary of $450.00, partial health insurance, and living accommodations on the hospital grounds. No prior interview was necessary, and they agreed to a starting date after I re-entered the Unites States. Apparently the need to fill the position was so critical that the process was quite simple.

The next step seemed to be the most difficult. How could I obtain a permanent visa, or so called *Green Card?* I visited the immigration office and spoke with an official who indicated that I should consult an immigration lawyer to facilitate the process.

"I don't think I can afford a lawyer," I told her.

"The other alternative is for you to return to your country and apply to the American Embassy there; or you could go to the embassy in Canada or Mexico."

"How long will it take to obtain the visa?" I inquired.

"Only a few days since you already have a student visa. Two weeks at the most." "What documentation will I need?" I wanted to know.

"You'll need your present visa, your Argentine passport and a copy of your birth certificate. Since they're all in Spanish, you're better off going to Mexico. You'll save some money as they don't need to be translated into English," the official continued.

"Why do I need to leave the country? Can't I do it right here?" I countered.

"The immigration law stipulates that in order to change your visa you must leave the country for at least 24 hours before re-entering. You can go to any city across the border." "May I have an application then?" I requested.

"No, you need to apply at a US embassy anywhere in Mexico." "What would hiring a lawyer do for me?"

"He'll do all the paperwork, and then you just have to leave the country for 24 hours."

"How much will a lawyer charge?"

"I couldn't tell exactly, maybe three or four hundred dollars. I could recommend one if you wish."

I thanked the woman and left. The wheels in my brain were turning. An intern at the hospital was from Mexico City. Maybe he knew someone in Mexico who could help.

The next day I found the intern working on the medical floor. I shared all the information about the process of changing my visa. Lorenzo agreed to meet after work to discuss the situation. When we spoke, I found that Lorenzo had a brother in Mexico City who practiced neurology. Lorenzo offered to contact him to see what he might be able to do.

A few days later Lorenzo let me know that his brother was willing to assist me with the necessary arrangements and had already recommended a moderately priced hotel. Lorenzo had written down his brother's name, Oscar Mendez, along with his address and phone number.

I was pleased. My plan was shaping up. The biggest obstacle was obtaining the money necessary for plane fare, hotel, meals, and incidentals. None of my friends at the hospital were in a position to float me a loan. Everybody lived on a tight budget. I thought of contacting Enrique, but quickly discarded the idea. Then I thought of our Argentinean friends who owned the luncheonette. They were in good shape financially and could perhaps advance me the amount I needed. I concluded that $300 would be enough, but first I had to check the price of the plane fare to Mexico City.

Securing a loan from Ricardo and Manuel at the luncheonette was not as difficult as I had anticipated. I gave them a detailed account of my plan and the expenses involved. They asked where I would live in the interval between my return and the starting date at Gardner State Hospital. I'd thought of two options. I could stay either at the hospital in Harlem or with my friend Fernando Astigueta at Bellevue Hospital. It was general knowledge that there were always unoccupied rooms or extra beds in the interns' and residents' quarters. It was customary for friends or visitors, male or female, to make use of those facilities. In addition, at either place I could wear my doctor's white jacket and go to dining hall with no questions asked. They also asked about repayment of the loan. I assured them that after two or three months working, I would have sufficient funds to pay them back. Ricardo and Manuel agreed to lend me the money as soon as I was ready to leave for Mexico.

I had capitalized on two facts. First, medical doctors in Argentina were held in high regard and inspired a great deal of trust. Second, Ricardo and Manuel were very appreciative of the way Enrique and I had helped them out, not only behind the counter, but also in solving minor medical problems.

Returning to the hospital I was satisfied with the crystallization of my plans. I had the capital needed and the connection in Mexico City. The job at Gardner State Hospital would be waiting for me upon my return. My next move was to cut short the internship by resigning. I planned to wait until after payday on a Friday, then I would have whatever I could save until then, plus the amount of the last check.

I had waited to tell Sylvia of my plans. I could have approached her for help but knew it wouldn't be fair to borrow money and then leave her. Her father was a lawyer in North Carolina who sent her money regularly. I could never understand why she worked at Harlem Hospital.

She could have easily done so much better elsewhere. It never occurred to me that she thought so too, and that our relationship had been step one of her vision. I knew it wouldn't be easy to tell her my plans; we had a very close relationship, and she'd helped me in many ways. I felt genuine regret and even guilt, though we had made no long-term commitments. But the time had come to move on. Sylvia wept with overwhelming sadness when I finally told her. "I'll call you when I get back," I said lamely, but we both knew, for us, it was the end. She did not fit in my plan to move temporarily to Massachusetts, and then return home.

After all these years there are still times when I reminisce about our time together and acknowledge my gratitude for all her help.

I realized that I had not been alone in my quest. A number of friends had come through and buoyed me in different ways when I was challenged by adversity.

I reassessed the situation. All the pieces were in place, it was time to take the leap. I presented my resignation, effective in two weeks. The director was furious. He drove home the point that I was breaking a legal contract, and this could bring consequences if I ever tried to return to the States.

"I will notify the Immigration Department. Your student visa will be revoked," he fumed. I did not explain any of my plans. I left the director's office with a smile on my face, and not a shred of guilt about terminating the free labor *my internship* had provided the hospital. I deeply resented this place that had offered me so little opportunity to grow. The last piece had been placed in the puzzle. *Mexico, here I come,* I smiled.

I purchased the airline ticket from my friend Luis, marveling at the good price that had somehow been negotiated for me. The morning was cold and rainy as I boarded the Aero-Mexico flight, and left New York City and the United States.

Weeks later I was on my way back. I arrived in the border city of Nuevo Laredo after traveling for almost 18 hours on *El Expreso,* a Mexican trans-border bus line, from Mexico City. Three hours later, I finally boarded a Pan American Airline plane to Houston, Texas and re- entered the United States with my newly issued *green card.* A connecting flight brought me to my final destination, New York City.

During the long hours of the trip, I frequently thought of my family back home. I had sent them a postcard from Mexico City. Since leaving Argentina, I had corresponded with my family on an almost weekly basis. They were aware of my general plans, but not of the details. They knew I was in the process of building some capital in order to return to Buenos Aires and open a surgical practice. In their letters they encouraged me to pursue my goals, wishing me a safe return. I valued their support more than if it had been a chest filled with gold. I had never mentioned the *Clinica Bazterrica* or the invitation to participate.

I had agonized over exactly what to tell them. How could I share the story of all that had happened to me in

America? I was trying to protect them from any emotional distress. It would have been unfair to worry them. The process of communicating with them matured me, deepening my understanding of what they meant to me, and how they were connected to what I wanted my future to be.

I reached Manhattan in mid-afternoon. I was physically tired from the long trip, but emotionally animated, determined to finish getting everything organized. I headed for the Port Authority, and at the information desk, I inquired about bus schedules for Gardner, Massachusetts. There was an express line with a stop in Worcester, and then a local route with a stop in Gardner, a trip of about five hours, leaving at 9:00 a.m. I wrote the information on the back of a brochure and put it in my pocket. From a payphone at the terminal I called my Mexican friend Lorenzo, letting him know I was back in the city. I also asked if there was lodging space in the interns' quarters and was relieved that there were empty rooms.

With my precious suitcase in tow I headed for the subway station in the direction of Harlem. Snowbanks and biting wind gusts were in stark contrast to the warmth and soft breezes of Mexico City.

Over the next few days I visited friends, spent an evening at the luncheonette, and informed Gardner State Hospital of my impending arrival. I thought of calling Sylvia but immediately dismissed the idea. I thought of her because, of the many friendships I had made here and would keep, hers had been the most intimate. I wanted to say goodbye in some meaningful way, but it wouldn't be fair to give her the impression I wanted to rekindle a relationship that I could not reconcile with my long term plans.

Long term plans were possessing my entire thought process. It did not occur to me that crucial changes might lurk ahead. Destiny and unexpected circumstances would derail my present intentions, eventually leading me to a secret double life involving the security of the United States. The same country I was plotting to leave, disillusioned and discontented.

As soon as I had boarded the Aero-Mexico plane for the flight to Mexico City, I relaxed. It was such a relief not to struggle to find every word or phrase needed to express my thoughts. I could communicate freely once again. Deplaning in Mexico City, I easily read all airport signs and understood the announcements the loudspeakers blared, naturally overhearing the conversations of fellow travelers around me. The signs directed me to a taxi stand outside the main entrance where I gave the driver the name of the hotel recommended by Lorenzo's brother. During the ride, I lounged in the back seat with my companion suitcase by my side and conversed with the driver, not because I felt talkative, but to refresh my Spanish.

After settling into the hotel room, I telephoned Oscar Mendez at his office to announce my arrival and arrange a meeting. Oscar graciously invited me to dinner. Not yet familiar with the transportation system, I opted for a taxi ride, giving the cab driver the address supplied by Lorenzo. We soon arrived in front of an elegant house in an upper-class neighborhood.

Seated at the dinner table were Oscar's parents and his younger sister Lucia. During the easy conversation I learned that this was the paternal estate. Oscar had his own home at his clinic. His office occupied the street floor level, and consisted of a waiting room, the receptionist/secretarial station, four examining rooms, and a laboratory/x-ray area. Oscar's spacious bachelor's apartment sprawled across the second floor.

At dinner, I was the center of the conversation, answering many questions about Argentina, my professional goals, and my experiences in New York City. I was cautious not to paint too negative a picture of the internship, not knowing how much information Lorenzo had shared about conditions at Harlem Hospital.

Oscar offered to meet with me the following day after hours, providing directions to the U.S. Embassy so I could initiate the process of obtaining a permanent visa. The next morning, after a continental breakfast in a café near the hotel, I headed for the embassy. There I felt self-assured enough to be able to ask for the Office of Immigration in English though I quickly reverted to Spanish after the initial introduction. They gave me a five-page application printed in Spanish to fill out, which I completed and presented together with my Argentine passport imprinted with the stamped student visa. To my dismay, they charged a fee of 25 American dollars for the application process, which I paid in cash at the Treasury Office next door, as instructed. There, I was stunned to be informed that a personal interview would be scheduled in about six weeks after the background check was completed. Almost in shock, I asked, "How long will it take for the visa to be issued after the interview?"

"After the personal interview, about two or three more weeks," responded the clerk. "If everything checks out all right, that is." I gave Oscar's office phone number for notification of the interview's date and left the embassy thoroughly agitated, going over in my memory the protocol described in New York, comparing it to the actuality of what had just happened. I was quite upset. I had been told, "It will be a matter of a few days... two weeks maximum."

I began to walk off my anger. I needed to collect my thoughts and plan for the unanticipated delay. Already running short of funds, I would certainly not be able to survive another ten weeks or more. I swore under my breath, feeling powerless and deceived yet again. Back in the hotel room, I paced the floor, reminding myself that I wasn't the type to quit at the first sign of trouble. Late in the afternoon I called Oscar who offered to meet for dinner at 10:00 that evening, a customary dining hour in Latin countries. I politely declined, asking if we could meet right after his office hours to discuss some problems I was facing. Oscar suggested the Rivoli Café, within walking distance of the hotel.

I felt juvenile having to dump my problems on Oscar. I hardly knew him, but I knew no one else in Mexico City either. Like it or not, I would have to share my situation. I could think of nothing else to do.

Seated at a window when Oscar arrived, I blurted, "Oscar, I'm in trouble." "What's going on?" he frowned.

I related the embassy story. "I need to stay longer than anticipated, another ten weeks or so, and I'm running short of funds".

We ordered two coffees and put our heads together.

"You need to move out of the hotel and find a *pension,"* Oscar said.

In Latin countries, and some places in Europe, a *pension* is a favorite living place for students. Families commonly rent extra bedrooms at a modest price which also includes breakfast and dinner.

I agreed that it made sense. "Tomorrow I'll check ads in the newspaper." "Try *El Diario Universitario.* Most pensions advertise there."

We thrashed out other aspects of the situation until Oscar excused himself. He had a consultation at the hospital, he said, leaving the café.

I mulled over everything we had discussed on the walk back to the hotel. It was clear that I needed to earn some money. *I could tutor students in English*, I joked bitterly to myself.

THE UNINTENTIONAL IMMIGRANT

I sat in the hotel lobby deep in thought. I would have to budget my money like a miser or pauper. No more taxis or big meals. In the room, I examined my *bank*, the envelope in the suitcase containing my money. Inside the envelope was the plane ticket, too. I had an idea. As a last resort, I could cash in the return flight and go back by bus. *Something to think about*, I reflected.

First thing the next morning I bought a copy of *El Diario Universitario* where I found, in the *Hospedajes* section, several pension ads. After copying the address and telephone number of four of them, I went down to the front desk to get some help navigating around the city. The clerk showed me a map and located each pension.

I asked the clerk to point out Oscar's clinic location. There were two other pensions close by. I might as well try them. I made the necessary phone calls and arranged visits. I chose a pension owned by a single older lady and her daughter. I would be the sole guest. I paid the rent in advance for the first week. The amount equaled three days at the hotel, and meals were included. I moved in around noon the same day. The room was clean and pleasant with an adjoining bath for my use only. That evening I sat at the dinner table with the owner and her daughter, both friendly. I was satisfied with my choice. Now I needed to consider finding some sort of work to support myself in case the permanent visa process was delayed.

Now, I had nothing to do but wait for word from the embassy for the interview. I decided to assume the role of a tourist. Over the next two days I wandered around the city, admiring its colonial architecture and historical sites. I spent considerable time in *El Zocalo*, the central plaza, the size of six city blocks. On Saturday morning I heard from Oscar, who invited me to meet some friends and participate in a typical *Mexican Serenata*. When I arrived at his place, his friends were already there.

They included Arlene, Oscar's girlfriend; a recently married couple, Emilio and Perla; and Alberto with his fiancée. The seven of us took two cars to another part of the city where we met a Mariachi band consisting of four musicians. From there the whole group marched to a colonial home with a white façade and a red tile roof.

Stopping under the balcony, the Mariachis started playing their instruments and singing while the rest of the group loudly expressed their well wishes to Marleen, the owner's daughter, celebrating her 21st birthday. Oscar had planned the entire scenario to introduce me to this girl, who would be my companion for the evening. Marleen appeared at the front door beaming and surprised. Gracefully she invited everyone in. We spent the evening on an interior patio, singing, dancing and enjoying each other's company.

Marleen's parents provided wonderful Mexican specialties including appetizer tacos, a variety of enchiladas, and beverages to make their daughter's celebration a complete success. I couldn't hide my delight in meeting the jovial, dark-haired Mexican beauty. On our way home, I was at a loss for words to show my appreciation for being included in Oscar's circle of friends. Before parting, Oscar mentioned that he would pick me up at the pension early in the morning, as we were going for a picnic to Cuernavaca, a well-known resort town a few miles from the city, famous for its pleasant and warm weather all year around. "Of course, Marleen will be your date," he said with a wink. The festivities continued with more celebrations and family dinners at Marleen's and at the Mendez Estate.

Over the next few weeks, we visited sites in the city, the Aztec ruins, and drove to Taxco, an artist's community about 100 miles south of Mexico City. Taxco is known for manufacturing silver jewelry and artifacts. My stay was turning out to be a great vacation.

As the sun lazily leaned to the west one bright Sunday afternoon, I received a call from Marleen. The group was planning an evening of fun at the Xochimilco Gardens. Xochimilco, meaning flower field in the Aztec language, is an area on the outskirts of Mexico City with a maze of canals remaining from the antique waterways used as a transportation venue for supplies and merchandise in the pre-Hispanic period. It is now a popular romantic escape for groups of young locals.

Upon our arrival, Marleen, Oscar, and friends rented one of the many colorfully decorated barges to leisurely float through the canals accompanied by a hired Mariachi band. The spacious gondola-type *trajinera,* painted with a symphony of vivid colors, had arches of fresh flowers as a roof. Long tables with numerous chairs made it ideal for eating and drinking while being poled amongst the flowered islands.

Under a moon-lit sky, caressed by the warm night breeze and surrounded by the intoxicating aroma of flowers, Marleen and I felt as close to a romantic interlude as we ever had. The soothing rhythm of the Mariachi music and the tropical drinks lulled our inhibitions, but we refrained from allowing the inevitable yearning to merge bodies and souls.

At the end of the tempting evening, at Marleen's front door, we parted with a simple, "Good night" but the intense magnetism between our gazes confirmed our mutual regret at parting.

For days, I questioned my true feelings. How firm was my conviction to follow the path of Gardner State? Was I ready to derail my plans and stay in Mexico City? *Not to decide* is a way *to decide.* Eventually, the uncertainty faded into the recesses of my unconscious.

In about another two weeks of stretching my money, I found myself short of funds. Consulting Oscar about the problem, we decided to find employment for me. Because of the nature of his practice, Oscar didn't have a place for me in his clinic, but he knew of an older general practitioner looking for a younger doctor to join him in his practice. Oscar contacted him and they arranged for me to function as a temporary assistant for the next few weeks while the doctor looked for a permanent partner.

I would receive a modest stipend, more than enough to meet my needs. Hospital authorities never questioned this arrangement, which was a real puzzle to me. They knew I graduated from the University of Buenos Aires Medical School in Argentina, but nobody checked my credentials or inquired if I was licensed to practice in Mexico. Either the laws were very lax, or they just chose to ignore them.

After six weeks, a call came from the embassy notifying me of the interview appointment. A week later I received the long-awaited permanent visa.

Marleen and Oscar drove me to the bus terminal. The three of us embraced and said our goodbyes. Each of our faces was streaked with tears as the bus departed.

Marleen and I had understood each other and were able to communicate freely. As a result, we had developed a deep relationship based on trust. This friendship would last for years. There had been no romantic or sexual involvement, save for the one evening of *flower magic*.

Knowing my time in Mexico was brief, it had somehow seemed inappropriate for us to pursue more.

After leaving Mexico, I kept in close telephone contact with Oscar and Marleen. Two years later, I invited them to my wedding, but they were unable to attend. As time passed, I learned of Oscar's marriage and the births of his two little girls.

At one point, I received a surprise call from Marleen telling me she had been married for over a year and had recently given birth to a baby boy whom she had named Jorge.

Nostalgically, I remembered our Mexican interlude. It had been a wonderful time in my life despite the uncertainty of the visa. Our hearts had been completely open and the memories were joyful. *How much more could there have been to our friendship?* I wondered. I was honored and touched to know of little Jorge. Perhaps what we had refrained from acknowledging, even to ourselves, was that a strong bond had developed... strong as any my life had ever known.

Over the years Oscar and Marleen's phone calls became less frequent, and then ceased altogether. Years later, with my wife and two of our four children, seven and three-year-old girls, we visited Acapulco for a week's vacation. On our return trip, we made a four day stop-over in Mexico City. I was determined to try to find my old friends. I visited the hospital only to find new young faces. Some of the older doctors remembered Oscar Mendez who had moved his practice miles south of the city. I went to Oscar's parent's estate only to find new owners. I called on the old Spanish-style house with the red tiled roof. The new occupant couldn't supply any information regarding the whereabouts of Marleen or her family.

I was saddened and disappointed to know that that earlier time was lost except to memory, but the place in my heart reserved for my Mexican experience remains forever full.

CHAPTER FOUR

I got off the Trailways bus at the lean-to shelter that served as the stop. I was at last in Gardner. It was late in the afternoon but still sunny, although snow that fell the night before covered the ground two inches deep. Snowbanks from previous storms fringed the streets almost three feet high. Gardner turned out to be a small city nestled among sparsely settled hills half-way across the state between the chilly Atlantic Ocean and the up-state New York border.

The single cab of Gardner's taxi fleet was parked next to the bus stop. I walked over and spoke to the driver. "How far to the hospital?" I asked.

"Which one?" the driver countered cheerfully. "We have the Henry Heywood Hospital and Gardner State."

"Gardner State," I replied.

The driver took my suitcase and put it in the trunk while I opened the rear door and climbed in. "New in town?" he wanted to know. "Are you a doctor? Well, welcome to Gardner," he continued without giving me the chance to say a word.

"You'll like Gardner. It's a very friendly town, different from that big place you're coming from," he chatted on, jerking his head back over his shoulder toward the bus that he knew had come from New York City. In the short drive to the hospital on the outskirts of town, he provided continuous information concerning the ethnic background of the people, *good* places to eat, where to shop, etc.; a thorough tour encapsulated in the fifteen-minute ride.

As we drove onto hospital grounds, the driver pointed out the names of buildings and their functions. We stopped in front of Thompson Hall, a modern looking structure with white columns across the stately entrance that housed the administrative offices. He carried my suitcase into the large lobby and thanked me effusively when I included a tip with the fare. I walked across the lobby and through the open door of the office labeled, "Administrative Secretary." A middle-aged woman got up from her desk and walked toward me.

"I'm Dr. Jorge DeNapoli," I said, introducing myself.

"Welcome, doctor. We've been expecting you," she smiled. "Unfortunately, it's Friday, after four, and all the doctors have already left. I'll call Dr. Cordes at his home to let him know you're here. He's the superintendent and lives in one of the houses just down the street." She made the brief call and then continued, "While we wait, let me show you your office." We walked down a corridor, passing several doors marked with doctor's name plaques.

"Here we are, Doctor Danali." "DeNapoli," I politely corrected.

"I'm sorry. Dr. DeNapoli," she said, coloring ever so slightly.

The office was spacious with a window overlooking the parking area. It was furnished with an almost brand-new, light wooden desk, a black swivel chair, and two other leather chairs arranged in front, anticipating consultations. Stylish accessories were organized neatly including a black telephone and leather trimmed ashtray. A side table with a Dictaphone, a small matching bookcase, and several pictures on the walls completed the interior.

I was quite impressed. *A palace of a room,* I thought, compared with Harlem's cubbyholes.

"Welcome, Dr. DeNapoli," an affable voice thundered. I turned to find myself facing a tall, burly man, perhaps in his early sixties, dressed in a well-tailored gray suit. "Dr. Cordes, in charge of the hospital," he introduced himself as he thrust his hand out. "We were expecting you to arrive sooner," he added with a cordial smile.

"I'm sorry, Dr. Cordes. I was delayed in Mexico waiting for my visa," I respectfully replied.

"Don't worry about it. You're here now. Only one doctor covers over the weekend, but Monday you'll meet everyone at our daily staff conference. I'll have someone show you to your quarters," he finished, still shaking hands. He turned back toward the door with a hearty, "See you Monday."

"My name is Anne Marie, I'm one of the secretaries," said the woman from administration, interrupting my thoughts. "Let me introduce you to Grazina, she'll be your private secretary."

Private secretary? This is getting better by the minute, I thought.

Grazina was a short, plump woman of around 50 years, with brown hair, and a perfect completion. She was smartly dressed and wore stylish high heels.

Grazina began describing the doctors' routine work schedule to me when a hospital worker arrived to show me to my quarters. As she continued with her orientation, I learned that the medical staff included seven physicians: the superintendent, the assistant superintendent, a psychiatric clinical director, a medical director, and three staff psychiatrists, including me.

The medical director was an internal medicine specialist in charge of the medical building housing psychiatric patients suffering from both acute and chronic medical illnesses. He covered the medical building every night except for weekends. The rest of the hospital was covered by the other physicians, excepting the superintendent. Each psychiatrist was on call one night a week, two nights every five weeks, and one weekend – Friday night to Monday morning – also every five weeks. Working hours were 8:30 a.m. to 12 noon and 2 to 5 p.m. On Fridays all doctors left at 4 p.m. In comparison to life at Harlem, this was a very reasonable schedule. It was one delightful surprise after another.

Frank, the tour guide, walked me to *The Mansion*, a stately building a short distance from Thompson Hall. He was a member of the building maintenance department and explained that *The Mansion* actually was an old New England manor. The rest of the buildings having been constructed around it as the site became a hospital complex. The old home had been subdivided into three spacious apartments, which were recently renovated and furnished. I was to occupy one of the first-floor units. The head of the laboratory/x-ray department lived in the entire upstairs with his wife. The other first-floor space was temporarily empty.

The living quarters had been repainted in anticipation of my arrival. I tried to absorb the avalanche of information about *The Mansion* while we moved from the entrance to the apartment's front door, and then into the large living room with its dark wooden paneling, leather sofa, and two over-stuffed chairs. *English-style decor,* I mused, while looking at the ceiling-high bookcase and desk, fireplace, and heavy, carved-wooden mantel. Frank showed me the spacious bedroom with a double bed, mahogany dresser and side table with a lamp and telephone. A full bath and compact kitchen completed the living space. A door led from the kitchen to the rear hallway and rear entry.

I was delighted with my new home, feeling my humanity returning due to the solidity of the imposing buildings, the gracious grounds, but mostly by the very friendly people. After the tour I inquired about calling a taxi to return downtown. I needed a good meal. Frank offered to give me a ride on his way home which I readily accepted. He dropped me in front of *Sally's*, a small family owned restaurant on Main Street. "The food is very good here," assured Frank.

It was indeed, and after a satisfying supper I thought of wandering around downtown to look at the stores on the main street but headed for the taxi stand. In no time it got quite cold when the sun fully set. Obviously, I was not properly dressed for New England weather.

Johnny, the same cab driver that had taken me to the hospital earlier, greeted me with a big smile and a "Hello, doctor, kind of cold to be walkin' around. Goin' back to the hospital?" I nodded and got in. Johnny took a different route back. "So you can see another part of town," he explained.

I showered off my travels and went to bed. It had been a full day. As I began to fall asleep, I thought about spending the weekend exploring the hospital grounds and the downtown area. In the morning I realized I had nothing to eat for breakfast but remembered seeing a sign in the lobby at Thompson Hall pointing towards the staff dining area. I headed off in that direction and found the *Employees' Cafeteria*, where I ordered coffee and English muffins. Just a few nurses and other hospital employees were enjoying breakfast that Saturday morning. Finding an empty table, I sat down.

"Good morning, doctor," a cheerful voice spoke from behind my shoulder. "May I sit with you?" She introduced

THE UNINTENTIONAL IMMIGRANT

herself as Susan Young, the Nursing Supervisor in F Building; female admissions.

"You must be the new psychiatrist we've been expecting. I understand you'll be taking charge of my building," she added. Obviously, everybody already knew of my arrival, how I would fit into the schedule, and what my duties would be. We chatted a while as we finished eating.

"I usually don't work on Saturdays, but one of my nurses reported in sick and I'm covering for her," she explained before leaving. I inquisitively assessed my new surroundings. *Everyone is very welcoming*, I thought, looking around. The absence of black people was striking after my year in Harlem. I spotted Grazina sitting at a table on the other side of the cafeteria with a male and female nurse. I decided to walk over to say hello, and as I approached their table, Grazina and the nurses stood up, a sign of respect that had never occurred at Harlem.

"Please sit down," I requested, joining them.

"I came in this morning for an hour or so to finish typing some reports for the staff meeting on Monday," explained Grazina, as she introduced me to the nurses. They then proceeded to fill me in on the lay-out and working arrangements of the hospital. I waited until they left to ask Grazina if she would mind giving me a ride to town after she finished at the office. "I would be delighted!" she responded.

On the ride, I learned that Grazina was married and the mother of two boys of college age. Her husband worked for the Heywood-Wakefield Company, a furniture manufacturing plant, the second largest employer in town. Gardner State Hospital was the largest. Her parents had emigrated from Lithuania and had lived in Gardner since before Grazina was born.

In the weeks and months ahead, she would come to be my main source of information about people, places, and happenings, both at the hospital and around town. I took to calling her my *Encyclopedia Britannica*. She could answer all the procedural questions, navigate me through the town and surrounding area, know where to get whatever I thought I needed, and fill me in on everything and everybody. As our professional relationship strengthened, I would come to rely on her a great deal, at times feeling as much like her adopted son as a professional colleague, just another one of her boys. Although she astutely maintained professional boundaries, ours was an easy relationship.

When Grazina dropped me in town that day, I curiously walked the three-block length of Main Street and the three blocks of the street that angled off one end. This L shape constituted all of *downtown*.

I stopped to shop at the local drugstore, buying toothpaste and shaving cream. While there, I met the pharmacist who instantly identified me as, "the new doctor at the State Hospital." I dropped in at the mens' clothing store, *Garbouse Brothers*, to look around, and bought a woolen hat. I badly needed other winter clothes, but would be short of funds until one or two pay periods had elapsed. As soon as one of the Garbouse Brothers realized I was the new doctor at the State Hospital, he offered to open an account for me. I politely declined. I ate lunch at the *Corner Diner* and took Johnny's cab back to the hospital. Still having encountered not a single black person.

While living in New York City, I had always used public transportation, but realized that to get around Gardner, I would need my own car. Otherwise, I would contribute a sizable portion of my pay to the friendly cabbie. On Sunday, I wandered the grounds of the hospital, spending the rest of the day organizing clothing and personal belongings in my new apartment. I was *settling in*.

The small city of Gardner seemed a friendly, livable place. I had certainly been welcomed and had no doubt my personal needs would be met. What I didn't know yet was whether there was a place for the new identity I was seeking that so far lacked definition. The loneliness of a true sense of place couldn't be ameliorated by a paneled living room, leather couch, or even the kindest word. But it was, I reminded himself, a good beginning, one for which I was very grateful.

If someone had questioned me, "a beginning for what?" I would have been at a loss to articulate my feelings. I only knew that the last year of my life qualified as a detour. I had felt like one of the passengers on the train leaving San Antonio Oeste to traverse the barren steppes of Patagonia, though the connection, if it really existed, was buried deep in my unconscious. I also harbored a residue of anger about having to work in the unhealthy hospital environment of Harlem and living among those cast aside by the mainstream of American culture. They lived with little hope, and I had begun to suspect it could be contagious. In Harlem people were segregated in ways I hadn't begun to truly understand, and whom I would judge harshly for a lot longer, not willing or able to ask meaningful questions about the socio-economic system they lived within. My feelings evolved as the years passed.

I was now facing a new chapter in my life.

For as long as I could remember, I had believed life was very much more. Ever since becoming fascinated by world history at the age young men embrace heroes, I had found mine in the history of Rome. I had, with great joy, wandered through the escapades of these long-ago relatives, knowing that although *my* people were unseen in the pages of the annals of the Roman Republic, I had been somehow involved, living the same geography. I had grasped the flavor of conquest and heroism, having read avidly the pages that chronicled how honorable men went forth and prevailed. My interest in world history never seemed to be more than a pleasant pastime in which I indulged myself and relaxed. I had never dreamed to what extent the history of man's exploits informed this one man's personal quest for his own identity. I did know I felt myself to be my family's adventurer.

Monday morning at the first staff meeting, I was welcomed cordially by the professional staff and formally joined the medical group. Robert Renoux, one of the staff psychiatrists, offered guidance and assistance. He'd been on call over the weekend and presented for discussion and disposition three cases admitted to F Building, the female treatment section.

They also discussed cases to be discharged, patient's medication plans, follow-up, and housing, whether at home or in a group setting. The discussion was open, professional, and scientific. All doctors participated, which was to my advantage as it provided valuable insight into the mechanics of the psychiatric field which was new to me.

After the meeting, Doctor Schaffner, the assistant superintendent, took me on a tour of the different buildings, introducing me to nurses and personnel as we progressed. The last building we entered was F Building, which had been assigned to my charge.

Susan greeted me with a warm smile. "I'm looking forward to assisting you," she said with a comfortable blend of friendliness and professionalism. I also met three other nurses, one of them young and very attractive. I was not missing any of the details of the tour.

"Stay here and get acquainted with personnel and routine, doctor. Mrs. Young will be of great help with all the details.

Then meet me in my office after lunch to discuss other aspects of your duties," Dr. Schaffner said before leaving.

Day by day, I learned patient names and diagnoses, familiarized myself with psychiatric medications, treatment approaches, and how patients' degrees of progress were quantified. I spent considerable time in the hospital library updating my basic knowledge of psychiatry. I also enrolled in two evening courses at Boston University starting in the spring and registered for lectures at the psychiatric department of St. Elizabeth's Hospital. These future trips to Boston would allow me to become familiar with the city and its many cultural resources.

I was happy and comfortable in my new surroundings. Everyone I met, whether at the hospital or in town, was welcoming. I felt appreciated and valued. The easy, open way people shared information facilitated my adjustment and integration into the multifaceted, and soon to learn, the multi-ethnic society of Gardner. It felt like an entirely different country from my last placement.

Gardner had a population of almost 19,000 inhabitants, mostly of French-Canadian descent, with a significant number of Lithuanian and Polish heritage as well. Sunday afternoon dances at the Polish Club were well attended, especially by young adults from Gardner and nearby towns. I attended frequently and received frequent dinner invitations to the doctors' homes and others to attend family and social events, which greatly expanded my socializing.

I had at last discovered *the other America*, the one I had gleaned from portrayals in American movies, pictured and written about in its magazines, the only America perceived and acknowledged by many comfortable middle-class Americans in the 1950s. It was quite a contrast from the America I had fled.

Grazina showed me the announcement in the *Gardner Gazette* under *Local News: Jorge DeNapoli, MD, a native of Argentina, trained in New York City, has joined the staff at Gardner State Hospital. Dr. DeNapoli, who is unmarried, plans to reside on the hospital grounds.* I smiled inwardly as I read between the lines: an eligible bachelor is in town.

Administration relieved me of weekend duties for the first month. On my second weekend, I boarded the bus to visit friends in New York City with the idea of purchasing an automobile. I knew an acquaintance and fellow countryman who was the owner of a small used car dealership in the Bronx. I had spoken with him in anticipation of my visit to the City, asking about the possibility of buying a car at an affordable price. Luis, the owner, had assured me that he had a good automobile for sale, well within my means. On my trip back to Massachusetts, I drove my first car, a 1954 Pontiac. A gray 4-door sedan, which I had bought for $800, to be paid for in monthly installments.

CHAPTER FIVE

Spring was in the air. Buds glowed with color and the blurring of the branches tips far above hinted at new leaves ready to burst forth. The first green shoots of spring bulbs promised the cold's end. Snow had melted away. I welcomed warm breezes with relief and felt the warmth of spring rising in my spirit, too. I had casually dated several women from town and the hospital, but deliberately avoided allowing these trysts to become serious emotional involvements. The plan was very clear: to return to Buenos Aires within a year or two. I had had my fill of complications.

I very much enjoyed walking about the grounds of the hospital and nearby surroundings during free time. On one of these walks, I met a charming, talkative woman who offered to walk along with me. In the next thirty minutes I learned Margotte was the director of activities, in charge of facilitating patients' interaction as a method of improving their social skills. I also learned that she was in her early fifties, and had lost her husband, Dr. Zarkowski, two years before. She still lived on the grounds, in the house she had shared with her late husband, who had been a member of the hospital psychiatric staff. Their two children, a boy and a girl, were grown and married, and Margotte eagerly awaited the arrival of grandchildren.

On frequent occasions Margotte *coincidentally* met me in my walks. It soon became obvious that these encounters were planned. This flattered me and aroused my male curiosity. Our friendship soon grew from friendly to mutually seductive. One evening she phoned, inviting me to come over for wine at her place. Choosing the darkest path, I went to her house. She opened the front door dressed in a provocative low-neck blouse exposing her cleavage.

"I am glad that you accepted my invitation," she said, gesturing for me to enter. We sat on the living room couch next to each other. Two glasses and a bottle of white wine sat on the marble coffee table before us.

"How could I resist your many charms?" I asked with a smile. She responded by moving closer so our bodies made contact. I put my arm around her shoulders and bent to kiss her passionately. As the wine flowed and the night unfolded, our months of flirtation ignited into passion. After this initial encounter, we decided to meet in Boston to avoid any possibility of hospital employees discovering our liaison. We wanted our relationship to remain secret.

I would attend classes and conferences in Boston, and after we would meet in a hotel for dinner and *dessert*. Margotte's husband had left her comfortably situated financially, allowing her to cover the expenses of dinner, a room, and occasional theater tickets. It was a lovely affair for us both, but as time went by, Margotte became increasingly possessive and demanding of my time and attention.

As I became more and more aware of the hidden costs of this arrangement, I struggled to extricate myself, becoming less and less available to Margotte's calls by refusing her insistent invitations. It was unpleasant and a bit scary professionally to withdraw from what had become more of an entanglement than recreational fun, but eventually she realized it was over, and left me alone.

Although she was twice my age, I never made a connection between my relationship with Margotte and with Aunt Julia.

Could my intimate relationship with Aunt Julia years ago account for my attraction to older women? Or was it just coincidental?

Aunt Julia was one of the younger of my mother's ten siblings. Today, she is the only survivor of them all, living independently at age ninety-five. We frequently communicate by phone, and exchange greeting cards at Christmas, birthdays, and other special occasions.

When Aunt Julia was in her early thirties, recently divorced after a just few years of an unsuccessful marriage, and having no children, she moved next door to her unmarried oldest sister who made her living by running a small bed and breakfast in her own home.

Aunt Julia was an attractive woman with a shapely figure, light brown hair, and beautiful green eyes. My family visited them often since they lived a short ten blocks from us. We got together for frequent gatherings. It was during these times that I began noticing Aunt Julia acting in a rather seductive manner whenever we were alone. She would greet me with a tight hug pressing her breasts against my chest and kissing me near my lips. During family meals she would sit next to me rubbing her leg against mine, or furtively taking my hand beneath the table. At first, I thought it was only my imagination, but soon her overtures became impossible to dismiss.

At seventeen, hormones surged through every vein in my body. I couldn't understand how she could be attracted to a tall, skinny kid only half her age, but my ego was, of course, flattered. I was also painfully indecisive as to what my response should be. After all, she was my mother's sister, even though my mother was much older.

I decided to confide in my two best friends and seek their advice, hoping I would hear words that would give me permission to dismiss my guilt. Both were of my same age and we were in our senior year of secondary education at the *Incorporado Mayo,* a moderately priced, private academy. We took night courses, since the three of us worked days to pay for our schooling and to make some spending money. Edmundo Spollansky worked in his family's housewares' business in the Jewish district of Buenos Aires. Ricardo Pezman assisted in his father's heavy machinery shop.

My job was as a messenger boy in the financial district. I was the proud owner of a used bicycle, a gift from one of my uncles. I spent my days dodging the heavy downtown traffic delivering the business documents for my employer, an investment agency.

On the evening of the fateful discussion the three of us met after school, as we often did, in a nearby bar for refreshments. After presenting *the situation* and a short discussion, we combined the wisdom of our 17 years, and ruled that this would not be *incest* in the court of public opinion. They determined that I should respond to her presumed sexual advances. Ha!

What wonderful friends!

I agreed I would implement their biased sound advice, but deep inside I was frightened, unsure of my ability to have sex with any experienced adult, never mind my own maternal aunt. Months before, I'd had a couple of clumsy sexual encounters with a girlfriend, and another with a *call girl* arranged by my 20-year-old brother to break me into manhood. In each case, I had gone through the motions successfully, though my insecurities and inexperience prevented any emotional satisfaction.

The opportunity to carry out my friends' advice came at a family celebration on, of all days, my parents' wedding anniversary. All such events were held at my aunts' home, because she lived in a two-story single house with an ample kitchen and a large living/dining room area. Sometime into the family party, Julia suggested we go up to the third floor-terrace to view the progress of construction in on one of the tallest buildings in the city, only a few blocks away. My heart began to pound and my hands got sweaty. Looking back, at that point, what I really felt was just plain fear. Once on the terrace, Julia wasted no time before taking me into her arms, and passionately kissing me. I responded as well as I knew how. We engaged in heated foreplay without actually consummating the act.

We agreed to meet at her house a few days later, when the older aunt would be away for the afternoon doing some shopping. This was the beginning of a beautiful relationship with mutual emotional and sexual satisfaction. We had frequent encounters in Julia's place whenever her sister was absent. The affair continued for about a year until she met Paul, who eventually became her second husband. Julia and I never discussed ending our affair; it just faded away without any negative emotional residue. Amazingly, my new uncle became a close friend and a strong paternal figure in my life. Their marriage lasted happily for more than forty years, ending only with Paul's death.

During all of the intervening years, even up to this present day, my aunt and I have never spoken of our intimate relationship, but on many occasions, our eyes met and shared the warmth of deep affection. Our relationship was an *on the job training course* in sexual maturity, helping me make the transition from a sexually inadequate adolescence to a graduate with a *manhood* major. The suitcase that she gave me as a departing gesture and as a token of our intimate affair was symbolic of my graduate diploma, sending me out into the world equipped with invaluable experience.

For a decade after arriving to this country, the suitcase accompanied my steps, and I attached to it the aura of a personal talisman. Then, a friend borrowed it to travel abroad, the airline misplaced it, and it was never to be found. Sometimes, when absorbed in thoughts of times past, I envision my suitcase, dusty and alone, forgotten in the Lost and Found area of an abandoned airport in some remote corner of the world… waiting.

After extricating myself from the emotional demands and professional risk that Margotte presented, I devoted most of my energy to immersing myself in daily work. I was gradually becoming a productive member of the psychiatric team, relating well to the doctors, nurses, and hospital personnel. I was devoted to my patients, treating them with respect and compassion. In a few short months, I had become an asset to the hospital psychiatric community. I had gained the esteem and appreciation of those interacting with me, made several good and trusted friends, and was proud of being part of their lives. On my incursions into town, I was always treated cordially with welcoming smiles. People, even strangers, would stop to greet me and chat. Invitations to functions and community events were frequent.

I felt comfortable and emotionally fulfilled in this new home. I had become a *de facto citizen* of this new America. For the second time I felt I belonged to a community as a professionally respected adult. Surprisingly, the other time was during my *Mexican experience.*

CHAPTER SIX

As soon as I had become integrated into the professional climate of F Building. Susan, the head nurse with whom I had developed a warm professional relationship began to frequently suggest that I should date the pretty nurse who'd caught my eye on that first tour of the building. I had never failed to notice when that nurse was near, following her with my eyes as she walked by. I was always extra nice when I had the occasion to speak with her. She in turn always had smiling eyes for me.

Her name was Dolores I. Boudreau. *Obviously French,* I thought. Susan had noticed my interest from the first, and as spring approached, I was aware that my thoughts stayed with Dolores after each chance encounter. I watched for her as soon as I came into the building. One Friday when Susan was attending a nursing staff meeting, Dolores accompanied me while making rounds. I seized the opportunity to ask her for a date.

"I was planning to go to Worcester tomorrow. Would you like to be my guide? If you are not busy of course." I wasn't surprised when she said yes. But there was a problem: my car was in the garage for repairs.

"Do you think we could use your car? Mine is being repaired. You could pick me up at my place," I continued, feeling foolish with this bold request. To my delight she agreed.

Saturday dawned sunny and beautiful. We drove around the city and had lunch at a sidewalk café. As we strolled through a downtown park, I casually reached for her hand and she squeezed back. Sitting on a bench, smiling and looking into each others' eyes, we admitted our mutual attraction.

Now or never, I told myself, leaning over and stealing the lightest of kisses. She responded by pressing closer and kissing me warmly. We whiled away the afternoon kissing and holding hands, laughing and wandering about like a pair of teenagers.

Dolores Boudreau.

I told her about many of my first American experiences in New York City, tactfully skipping any mention of Sylvia and her help in improving my English. She talked extensively about her family. Her French-Canadian parents had immigrated years ago. All six of their children had been born in the Gardner area, Dolores being the oldest. She had four brothers, including one set of twins, and a sister, the youngest child. Dolores and I returned early in the evening, parked the car in front of the Mansion, and necked giddily.

After that first afternoon we dated frequently, and soon, *liking* turned to deeper feelings. I was content in a new way, Dolores was constantly in my thoughts, and, for the first time, I felt I was truly in love.

Susan had gradually become Dolores's confidant about our relationship. Susan was about ten years older, and her husband Roger, a car salesman and mechanic, were parents of a twelve-year-old son. As the four of us became increasingly friendly, we visited Susan and Roger's home more frequently. We dined out together and socialized quite often. Soon, we had become close friends. We took frequent day trips around the New England countryside, visiting quaint towns while exploring the Maine coast and the White Mountains of New Hampshire. We climbed Mount Washington, hiked through the forests and swam in the cold waters of snow-fed mountain lakes.

Dolores introduced me to her parents and siblings. I had been invited to dine with them as a formal introduction to the family. This was a very special occasion. Dolores's mother, an excellent cook and superb baker, spent hours in the kitchen.

As we sat down to eat the ambiance was expectant, with everybody on their best behavior. I was the focus of attention and guest of honor at the table that was set with special care. I eagerly but nervously awaited the meal. I usually enjoyed all food and every type of cuisine I had sampled. The only exception was ham, which in any form, turned my stomach. Out from the kitchen came Dolores's mother's truly impressive offering; a ham that would have fed the whole staff at the hospital, with pineapple slices and all the trimmings.

I knew the polite thing to do. I may not have been my most charming, but bite-by-bite and with tremendous effort I worked my way through the generous portion staring at me from the plate. Of course Mrs. Boudreau was exceedingly gracious, and, with savoir-faire, no sooner had I finished the last morsel on my plate, than she, beaming with satisfaction, sliced another pink slab of the infamous ham and presented it to me with a flourish. I painfully struggled through it once again. Thankfully, the desserts were delicious. The entire evening was an enjoyable event, except for the main course. I felt comfortable and happy relating to her parents and siblings.

I never mentioned my dislike for ham to Dolores. At my second dinner at her home, Mrs. Boudreau thought to repeat the success of our first meal together and cooked ham again. The third dinner featured ham as well. Finally, as tactfully as possible, I told Dolores of my true feelings about the choice of menu, which she passed on to her mother. From then on, every time there was a family affair that included dinner, Mrs. Boudreau would call me to ask my preference for dinner. You can be sure that ham never made its appearance again, for which I was very relieved.

Those first family dinners we shared have remained a source of laughter through the years, and as my presence at dinners and family gatherings increased, I progressively became part of the family.

As time passed and our relationship deepened, I found myself precariously perched on the horns of a dilemma. I was in love with Dolores and wanted to marry her, but I had a preconceived master plan that didn't fit in the scenario that was unfolding. I had become a prominent component of hospital life and a respected member of the community. I had been received with open arms and included as part of the Boudreau family. I had subtly become an *American* and I adored Dolores. Almost a year had passed since our first date and this felt like *my new life* to my core. Was I willing to give all this up in exchange for the uncertainty of starting anew in Buenos Aires? Argentina was experiencing political upheaval and a deteriorating economy that didn't bode well for a promising future. But family ties and friends left behind were factors to consider. I had never intended to leave them forever.

It would be unfair to burden Dolores with my conflicting and ambivalent feelings. She might question the strength of my love for her. For days I wrestled with contradictory thoughts.

On a duty-free weekend, I traveled to New York City to stay with Fernando at Bellevue Hospital and talk to him about this conundrum. After many hours of deliberating, my psychiatrically trained friend abruptly asked, "Jorge!" Do you envision spending the rest of your life with Dolores?"

I emphatically said, "Yes!"

"Then you have your answer. There is no need, *y first communto*, to continue speculating," replied Fernando, which ended the discussion.

Driving back to Massachusetts, I ruminated over the fact that I had known the answer all along. I arrived in Gardner late Sunday afternoon. Multicolor leaves announced the arrival of autumn. I stopped at Dolores's and invited her to go for a drink. At the local watering hole we sat side-by-side in a booth. Holding her hand I murmured, "I wonder if there will be a house available at the hospital after we're married." She smiled hugely, and with tears in her eyes she queried, "Are you proposing? Are we engaged? You haven't even talked to my father yet. He might say no!" We agreed not to mention anything to anyone except Susan. That night, lying in bed, I realized that I hadn't actually gotten an answer from Dolores. I picked up the phone and, without a thought about the time, I dialed her number.

"Well, is it 'Yes' or 'No'?" I said when she answered. "It's YES! Do you want it in writing?" she teased.

I'll have to talk to her father, was my last thought before falling asleep.

When I woke up, my heart was bursting with feelings of contentment and happiness.

Then, suddenly, reality exploded before my eyes.

Was it destiny or my own actions guiding me to a path that was not in my original plan?

When I had arrived at Harlem Hospital, and less when I moved to Gardner, I had not intended to reside permanently in the United States. Now, unknowingly or purposely blocked from my conscious recognition, I was metamorphosing into an immigrant... an *unintentional immigrant.*

Twice, coming back from a date with Dolores, I was ready to speak to her father, but he was already in bed. When the same thing happened the third time, I spoke up! "Dolores, you better wake him up! Otherwise we'll never get married!" I was sure he already knew what I wanted to talk about when he came out of the bedroom in his robe. We sat in the living room, joined by Dolores and her mother. With some hesitation I began the formalities. "We love each other and would like your permission to marry." His response caught me off guard.

"Are you Catholic?" Mr. Boudreau wanted to know. I wasn't aware why my religion was germane, so I ignored the question and proceeded.

"We would very much like to be together forever…" While expressing my intentions I tried to think what Mr. Boudreau could actually want to know by his question. Nothing in my experience had prepared me for it.

Mr. Boudreau interrupted, repeating the same question. "Are you Catholic?" This time I responded, "Yes, sir."

"Are you baptized?" continued Mr. B. "You know the church will require a baptismal certificate and proof of first communion in order to perform the ceremony."

"I was baptized and I made my first communion." Mr. Boudreau nodded in approval. "You both have my blessings."

I was surprised by the authoritative nature of the questioning. Even though I had been aware that the family had strong religious convictions, I had no notion of exactly what that entailed.

To break the tension, Mrs. Boudreau interceded, "Time to celebrate!" she said festively, getting out their best liquor and glasses. I sighed with relief. Mr. and Mrs. Boudreau toasted us formally, heartily wishing us all good things in our future.

Now I began to worry about my own family. I couldn't simply write or telephone my parents with such momentous news. I was confident they were ready to be joyous with me for this rite of passage, but I was also certain they would realize that this meant they would truly be losing a son and the news would be hard to hear. I was also aware that they could not afford to attend the wedding.

The trip to New York City to talk with Fernando was, after all, mostly about coming to terms with becoming an American. As happy as I was with Dolores, I would not have tried to make living in Argentina a condition of our marriage. Besides, Gardner had reassured me America was the place to be and to raise our children. At the same time, I knew marriage was saying a permanent goodbye to my Argentinean life. I didn't want to hinder her strong attachment to her family and devotion to her nursing profession.

I wanted to tell my parents in person, hoping that I could explain that my acceptance of an American life was not a rejection of my first family. I luckily had little financial concern about the expense of such a trip; the *Back to Argentina Fund* was at my disposal. By deviating from my original reason for coming to the US, I had, in fact, become the unintentional immigrant.

Susan phoned to alert me about a minor detail I had overlooked. She brought it to my attention that in the United States it was customary to surprise the bride-to-be with an engagement ring, and formally propose marriage when it was presented. I had been unaware of such formality. Custom was either different in Argentina or else I had never paid much attention to such conventions.

Attempting to mend this oversight, I went to the local jewelry store to get an idea of what would be appropriate. The owner was very attentive and efficient, showing me several engagement rings within my limited budget. Diamonds, quality, brightness, clarity, karats, white gold, yellow gold, platinum, ring size; all variables I was supposed to consider. Within the hour I left the jeweler's hopelessly confused. *Call Susan!* said a little voice in my head, and she came to the rescue with definite suggestions of what Dolores might like.

It all seemed like a feminine conspiracy to me, but I wanted to please Dolores. I ordered a ring in accordance with Susan's suggestions, to be paid for with a down payment, the balance would be remitted in monthly installments.

The changing season could not be ignored. Gusts of cold winds were denuding the trees of their multicolored leaves. Winter was on its way. Dolores and I were busy with arrangements for our wedding. The date had been set; April 26th of the following year. We talked at length about the reason for my trip to Buenos Aires. She understood my filial needs and the parental respect involved in notifying my parents personally.

The news of the coming wedding and my trip to Argentina spread quickly throughout the hospital community and the town. I had requested a three month leave of absence, readily approved by Dr. Cordes, along with his effusive congratulations. He would arrange for a house on Neighborhood Road, which was hospital property, to be available as our living quarters after the wedding. To comply with hospital policy that married couples shouldn't work together, Dolores would be assigned to A Building, the male admitting unit.

Because of new financial constraints resulting from the engagement ring, I chose to travel on a Liberty cargo ship that had six staterooms available for up to twelve passengers. It was far from being a luxury liner, but good enough for the price.

We took a day trip to New York City to buy the ticket. Dolores knew her parents would definitely veto an overnight stay for an unmarried couple. Ah well, *c'est la vie!* It was another example of integrating conventions: a more rigid form of Catholicism, a material component to commitment, and sexual freedom being regulated.

Snowflakes were falling on December 20th as Dolores drove me to the Greyhound terminal in Boston where I would board the bus to New York for the first leg of my journey and separation from her. The ship would leave the next day from a west side pier.

As soon as we left Gardner, I opened the small box containing the engagement ring and offered it to her. "Will you marry me?" I asked. Totally surprised and delighted she blurted, "Yes, of course!" Eyes twinkling she added, "It's too late to say no! We must go back to show it to mother," Without another word she excitedly turned the car around and headed back to Gardner.

Her mother was impressed with the choice of ring. Smiling, I took all the credit wondering if she knew Dolores and Susan had engineered the selection.

It wasn't an easy goodbye at the bus terminal. Conflicting feelings gnawed at me. I was pleased to be going to see my family after almost two years but saddened to leave Dolores for three long months. We kissed passionately, deeply locked in each other's arms, declaring our mutual love. As the bus began to pull away I waved a silent *au-revoir* until she disappeared from my sight.

CHAPTER SEVEN

The next day was the official start of winter in Gardner, and simultaneously the first day of summer in Buenos Aires. I walked down the pier alongside the huge cargo ship. The black letters on her stern read *PENELOPE* with her country of origin, *Greece,* printed below it. I climbed the narrow iron stairway to board the rust-stained ship, dragging along my faithful companion suitcase. And so began my *Penelope Odyssey.*

"Welcome aboard," was the greeting of the first officer at the top of the boarding stairway. A crew member escorted me to the assigned cabin, located amidships. It was spartan, furnished with two steel bunk beds firmly secured to the gray metal wall, a midsize table bolted to the floor, two chairs, and two lockers. My roommate was a single gentleman, too, informed the sailor. I placed my suitcase on the upper bunk to take possession of the sleeper. I arrived back on deck in time to watch other passengers coming aboard.

Within an hour the ship began to hum deep within, then giant lines as thick as my wrist were cast off, and we pulled away from the pier. The ship's bow jutted into the Hudson's current, moving downriver past the Statue of Liberty and into the Atlantic Ocean, headed south. Passengers lined up along the railing for a last look at the receding New York City skyline. They then greeted and introduced themselves. I met David who was to share the cabin for the length of the voyage.

An announcement proclaimed that all passengers were to congregate in the dining hall to meet with the captain and the other officers, to be welcomed aboard and go through orientation. After greeting and shaking hands with everyone in the group, the captain withdrew, leaving the first officer to instruct us. He gave a presentation describing the layout of the ship, the daily routine, and the expected itinerary. From the answers given to the many questions asked by the group, I learned that the *Penelope* was a *Liberty* cargo ship and a veteran of World War II, originally used to transport equipment and supplies to European war zones. After the armistice, the ship had been refurbished and modernized. The *Penelope* was 450 feet in length with five cargo holds and six cabins accommodating as many as twelve passengers. She sailed under the Greek flag, which meant a shipping company headquartered in Greece owned her. The crew consisted of the captain, six officers, and about thirty sailors. Our itinerary was subject to the demands of the cargo, which determined each port of call. The first stop would be Savannah, Georgia to unload farm equipment stored in the holds. One of the women inquired how long it would take to reach the port of Buenos Aires. She was told approximately thirty days.

The group disbanded to settle into their respective cabins. David was already there when I arrived at our room. He was a fellow Argentinean on his way to visit family in Entre Rios, a province north of Buenos Aires. David was 29 years old, living in Troy, New York, and employed by the Hudson Valley Community College as a Spanish instructor. I was not in the habit of disclosing personal aspects of my life and didn't mention being a psychiatric physician, making up the story that I was living in Boston working for a real estate agency.

I met the rest of the passengers at lunch who were seated around a large oval table securely bolted to the floor. The captain and officers occupied a neighboring table. In the passenger group there were five married couples, ranging in ages from late 30s to early 60s. Three of the couples were from Argentina, one from Uruguay, and the other from Porto Alegre, Brazil. All of them spoke Spanish. Seated at the table for the first time, the conversation centered on an exchange of personal background information; their children, jobs, and reasons for the voyage. It was more than I really wanted to know. David and I developed an instant friendship, perhaps because we were close in age, and felt apart from the *married* group. We spent the afternoon becoming familiar with the layout of the ship, moving along narrow passageways, up and down stairs leading to different deck levels, wandering into the engine room, and ultimately visiting the bridge. On our roaming we met some of the officers, the master engineer, and several crew members.

I was not accustomed to sea travel. Based on previous experiences, I would usually say, "I don't have the stomach of a sailor." Here was the opportunity to really find out. Sailing went well until we reached Cape Hatteras, when the seas caused a constant rolling of the ship.

Luckily I was able to tolerate it well. I tried writing a letter to Dolores but the movements of the ship made it nearly impossible. I had already written her three letters while on board, and a letter to my parents. I had an ample supply of writing paper and airmail envelopes. Shortly after boarding, I approached the officer in charge of ship-to-shore communications and spoke briefly with Dolores just after we left port. But it was rather expensive, as well as objected to by company policy, except in the case of business urgency or personal emergency. I settled for writing, planning to mail the letters from our ports of call.

As required by marine regulations, we practiced abandon ship drills weekly. On the first drill everyone on board was alerted to congregate next to their assigned lifeboat. We were to wear life vests and carry only important documents or personal valuables. I had brought with me an 8"x10" framed photograph of Dolores which I had hung next to my bunk bed. Running to the assigned lifeboat, I carried my passport, shoved my medical ID card in my pocket, and cradled Dolores's picture under my arm. Everybody laughed and thought it was cute but teased me about it for the rest of the voyage.

The passengers became a tight little community, conversing openly with one another and regularly taking all their meals together. David and I preferred to socialize with the crew, perhaps because of the age difference and marital status. It didn't occur to me that I was midway between David's status and the staid, married folk. I flirted with one of the women in her 40s, Laura, dismissing the notion of any romantic involvement on board only because of my fantasy of being thrown overboard by her irate husband. I enjoyed the warm thought, though, never wondering for an instant if my engagement to Dolores somehow made it inappropriate. I still felt single and free in accordance with my cultural background.

Most of the crew members, including three or four of the officers, comprised a young, heterogeneous group of diverse nationalities. They hailed from Greece, Columbia, Brazil, and several Caribbean islands; speaking English, Greek, Spanish and Portuguese. David and I soon became friendly with several Spanish speaking sailors and two of the officers. This group became our on-board community.

Late in the afternoon of December 24th we docked at the port of Savannah, Georgia. The captain had arranged, at the request of some of the travelers, for an excursion mini bus to pick us up at nine the next morning, Christmas Day, for a tour of the city. The *Captain's Christmas Dinner* was scheduled for nine that evening, shortly after the order of *lever anchors*. On Christmas Eve, with David and the crew, we went ashore visiting downtown, and then headed for the bars. For me, this was quite an experience. We drank, danced, and generally enjoyed ourselves in the company of ladies who were regular customers of the establishments. Crews from other ships joined in the fun, singing *song of the seas,* sea shanties and bawdy ballads, and relating stories of tempests and shipwrecks. We returned to quarters as the sun appeared in eastern skies. The captain's knock, announcing that the tour was about to leave, awoke us just as we had turned in. Not to miss anything or appear rude, we dragged our bodies onto the bus. Half asleep, we hardly noticed any of the sites nor paid much attention to the driver's commentary. I barely remembered to mail the letters. I tried to call Dolores from a public pay phone, but the long distance connection warned the wait could be more than an hour.

That evening the galley crew excelled in preparing a roasted turkey, the typical South American Christmas meal, which was enjoyed by all. Much partying took place among the

THE UNINTENTIONAL IMMIGRANT

group that evening, ending with David and me finding our way to the crew's dining hall where we continued to enjoy tropical beverages, laughs, and more fun.

The next morning sailing south from Savannah the crew buzzed around the main deck securing all movable objects. Rough seas were anticipated crossing the Caribbean on route to Puerto Bolivar on the Colombian coast where they scheduled to unload a shipment of coal.

During the feverish activity a fairly large container broke loose and fell on the legs of one of the sailors. He was rapidly transported to the cabin serving as the infirmary. I had witnessed the accident and couldn't restrain the medical urge to assist. Rushing to the infirmary, I identified myself as a surgical physician and offered my services. With the sailor trained in medical emergencies officiating as my assistant, we removed the sailor's clothing to evaluate the scope of the injuries. An extensive, deep laceration was unveiled on the right thigh and a visible fracture of the left lower leg. Using the available first aid supplies we immobilized the fracture by placing two narrow wooden boards on each side of the broken leg, wrapping it securely with an ace bandage to keep it in place. Wearing surgical gloves, I cleaned the large gash with saline solution and proceeded to inject a local anesthetic along the laceration, and then sutured the wound. The medic finished it by applying a tight bandage around the thigh.

The Greek sailor was grateful for the care. In broken English, smiling with knowledge of a secret now exposed, he said, "Thank you, fake doctor, you no sell houses." The news of the unfortunate accident spread rapidly through the ship. From then on I was respectfully called *Doc*, or teasingly addressed as, *Fake Doctor*, imitating the words of the injured sailor. When the ship arrived in Puerto Bolivar, the injured sailor received further treatment at the local hospital.

My cover being blown, I had to admit that I was actually a physician, training in the United States. I apologize to David for not disclosing the true facts, and he felt comfortable with my explanation. Fate kept offering instances to practice my surgical skills, while such opportunities were denied to me in American surgical circle.

The storm was not as intense as predicted. The rest of the crossing was accomplished with calm seas and sunny weather. Everyone who craved a nice suntan was pleased with the weather; I always searched out the shade to prevent my sensitive skin from painful sunburns. On our arrival in Puerto Bolivar a warm reception awaited us. Friendly vendors lined the pier offering local wares for sale and advertising places to visit; but the emptying of the holds and reloading of iron ore was accomplished in only a few hectic hours. The injured sailor returned to the ship sporting a fresh white cast as a souvenir for everybody to sign.

As the bright, orange sun slowly sank toward the horizon, the *Penelope* unhurriedly moved away from the coast of Colombia heading for Port of Spain, on the island of Trinidad. Days passed cruising toward our new destination.

David and I habitually spent a lot of time in the company of our sailor friends. The crew constantly chatted among themselves about whether David or I might be called upon to *ring the bell*. They were quite inventively mysterious about it, sometimes appearing to furtively change the subject when we came near, as though they hadn't wanted to be overheard. They avoided giving explanations concerning what the task might entail in spite of our persistent questions. Gradually our curiosity built up to such a crescendo that we practically demanded to know what this, *ringing the bell,* was all about. Obviously, the sailors had us where they wanted. Little enclaves would meet ostensibly to discuss the options and specific qualifications of the candidates in plain view and within hearing distance of both of us. David and I couldn't conceal our growing curiosity. This mischievous pastime went on for days. Bit by bit, the information tantalizingly surfaced that this bell ringing would take place at an unscheduled stop, unauthorized, but perhaps not unknown to The Company; somewhere after leaving Port of Spain and before crossing the equator. We worried and pondered about the task in every imaginable way. How difficult could it be, and how dangerous? What was the significance of ringing the bell?

The captain planned to dock at Port of Spain on the morning of December 31st, to celebrate the New Year in port. The festivities would be spectacular and interesting, he promised, combining local traditions with Caribbean flavor and British humor. Tourists were always an integral part of the fun. The ship's company, however, had other directives, ordering the captain to delay arrival as their cargo was not yet available. As a result, the *Penelope* celebrated New Year's Eve on the high seas to the dismay of passengers and crew.

The captain had organized a special dinner and dance in the passengers' hall, accompanied by to the throbbing rhythms of a record player. Champagne was provided for a midnight toast, rung in by the sound of the ship's horn announcing the stroke of midnight. Passengers hugged and kissed with well wishes for the coming year. Laura approached me with a smile, embraced me tightly and kissed me on the lips, then moved on to share wishes with others in the group. My ego took a quantum leap as I surreptitiously glanced about to locate her husband, wondering if our brief encounter had been witnessed. I sighed with relief at seeing him socializing at the other end of the hall.

I had had enough to drink that her kiss not only over activated my sex drive, but also clouded my judgment and loosened my inhibitions. I moved close to Laura and said, softly but boldly, "Meet me at the infirmary tomorrow morning at 11."

With a slight nod, she smiled a mute, "Yes." David and I continued celebrating at the crew's dining hall with alcohol flowing freely. I woke up a little hung over the next morning, quickly took a shower and headed for the infirmary in arousing anticipation of a romantic encounter. I had borrowed the keys from my friend the medic. It was almost 11 when I arrived. As the minutes passed, my hopes gradually evaporated.

Forty-five minutes later I climbed the stairs to the main deck to breathe the clean fresh sea air and to clear my head, thinking, *You win some, you lose some.*

In the early evening I joined the passengers in the dining hall. Laura casually walked by me, and without making eye contact, she said almost inaudibly, "Sorry, I couldn't make it." *Things happen for the best*, I thought, and for the rest of the journey I was polite and restrained when we crossed paths, until the last day on board.

When sailing into the expansive bay of Port-of-Spain, passengers were treated to the contrast of one of the most scenic ports in the Caribbean with the cosmopolitan skyline of the city's tall buildings. Three days had passed since New Year's. The city was quiet, but Latin music still filled the air. During our two day stay, we enjoyed the sandy beaches and visited the marshes crowded with many species of brightly-colored, tropical birds. Leaving the Island of Trinidad, the ship continued its journey, with suspense increasing, as David and I remained the target of frequent taunting regarding the now famous bell.

In the mid-afternoon of the second day of sailing, as the *Penelope* slowly inched closer to the coastline, the First Officer pointed to a rocky silhouette and identified it as Devil's Island. I realized we were approaching the shores of French Guiana.

During secondary school studies, my class had taken a field trip to Dutch Guiana and French Guiana. We stayed at Cayenne, the capital, and visited the former prisons on the mainland and on Ile Royale and Ile St. Joseph. We couldn't go to Devil's Island, as landing by boat was too dangerous due to strong cross-currents.

Leaning on the railing to admire the blue sea, I was still puzzled over what might be expected of David and me. Suddenly, an old joke came to mind that relieved some of the anxiety. As I remembered it, I burst out laughing.

Quasimodo committed suicide by jumping off the tower at Notre Dame Cathedral and a group had gathered around the body lying on the sidewalk when a gendarme arrived. Seeing an onlooker with tears in his eyes, he asked, "Did you know this man?" The onlooker responded, "Not really, but his face rings a bell."

We finally went ashore in the port town of Raundeau which was nestled into the surrounding hills, and green with lush vegetation. The town's common, just across from the pier, was a lovely park bordered with palm trees and tropical bushes blooming in vivid colors. A number of vendors sold fruit drinks and snacks, souvenirs, locally made T-shirts and colorful blouses. Townspeople walked about browsing and making purchases as they stopped at different booths. The passengers and some of the crew joined the locals, taking a stroll under the hot sun.

During our walk David and I came across a monument on one corner of the common. The mystery was unraveling. Under a wooden framed, pergola-like structure, hung a shiny bronze bell, apparently rescued from a shipwreck. A metal plaque written in French commemorated those lost at sea. Left to the imagination still was the meaning and subsequent events following the tolling of the bell, as well as how the townsfolk would respond to the visitor who carried out the task. We found out at dusk, as the sun set over the western hills, and night shadows began to creep across the side of the square opposite the pier.

"Time to ring the bell!" said a crew member as he grabbed David's arm and marched him toward the monument. All of us followed behind. The selection of the bell ringer had been finalized before they left the ship by drawing names randomly out of a coffee cup.

At exactly 7:30 p.m., David was commanded to ring the bell three times. At the sound of the bell the locals disbanded, strolling away from the day's festivities while the vendors collected their wares and emptied their booths. In a matter of minutes, the square was deserted. The other passengers decided to explore the town before returning to the ship. Dusk deepened quickly as night fell. We waited with the crew members to see what would happen next. In less than half an hour the area was pitch black, lit only by pale ovals thrown across the common from lamp posts along the periphery.

The darkness must have been some sort of a signal, for suddenly a dozen provocatively dressed women appeared, sauntering towards the group smiling and chattering in French.

Evidently, this was what the sailors had been anticipating. They socialized with the ladies who were now speaking English and Spanish, heavily accented with French. Our whole group wandered into a nearby cafe with a long bar and numerous tables and chairs. Obviously, we had been expected, as well-known good customers, from the friendly greetings of the owners and several locals seated at the bar.

One of the women sat down by me, beginning an easy conversation asking about my travels. I shifted the talk towards discovering more about the ritual that had just taken place. She related that they were working girls, coming from different cities in France. They came to Raundeau with the consent of the French government, to voluntarily stay for two or three years, for the purpose of earning a sizable fortune, which would allow them to return to France and lead fairly prosperous lives. Three to four ships a week made unscheduled stops at Raundeau, one of the main ports of call on the way to South America. *A rather profitable enterprise,* I mused.

After sharing conversation and a couple of drinks, I offered her a $10 bill for her social time which she took with a *merci* and a smile. She kissed me on the cheek as she left to sit at another table with a sailor. After all, she had a living to make. David was nowhere to be found. Hours later one of the sailors yelled, "Midnight," alerting everyone that it was time to report back. The *Penelope* was scheduled to sail at 1:00 a.m. This unscheduled stop in Raundeau for the benefit of the crew was the captain's show of appreciation for the loyalty and hard work they displayed during the trip. Apparently, this impromptu event was routine in all their voyages.

As soon as the ship left port, preparations began for the equator crossing ceremony; the festivities would begin the night before and last into the next morning. The crew had decorated part of the main deck with underwater related items, with a large crate serving as King Neptune's throne. The *Polliwogs* (those who had never crossed the line dividing the two hemispheres), had to undergo mild physical hardships and embarrassing ordeals ordered by King Neptune, played by a sailor, in order to earn their certificate. David and I had to wear clothing borrowed from the female passengers, while crew members sprayed us with shaving cream. The *Polliwogs* were then baptized by being completely soaked in sea water. King Neptune was dressed with a long red cape, a crown, and held a trident as his staff. He presided over the ritual.

Once the ceremony was complete, just as the ship passed over the imaginary demarcation line, the captain awarded the participants a *Certificate of Equatorial Crossing*. It was dated January 8, 1958. It was a really fun event marked with plenty of food and beverages to enhance the celebration. Singing and drinking continued through the night.

So far, I had tolerated the sea journey well. Occasional symptoms of nausea subsided with repeated doses of Dramamine. I had also helped David by providing him anti-seasickness medication as needed. But our well-being was shortly to be significantly affected by upcoming weather. Reports had alerted the captain that we were headed into treacherous waters. The next port of call was Aracaju, on the Brazilian coast, three days away.

As we sailed around Cabo de Sao Roque, a tropical storm pounded the east coast of Brazil. Once more, the crew moved into action securing crates and other objects on the main deck. Strong winds and high waves soon caused the ship to rock and roll from side to side. At the same time the seas lifted the ship the length of the keel. The main deck was swept by powerful waves. Passengers were advised to gather in the dining hall to be instructed about safety protocols. After the presentation, several of them returned to their cabins. It was difficult to transit the narrow passageways during the constant thrashing about of the vessel. David and I went to the crew's dining area where we felt safer. Crew members took turns performing the required preventive tasks. Those resting in the hall were talking cheerfully, joking about the storm and drinking coffee, ignoring the fury of the elements outside. It was obvious to them that we were very concerned about the safety of the ship. The cold sweat on our ashen faces was indicative of our intense physical distress.

At dinnertime only a few were seated at the table. The experienced sailors had advised me that eating some crackers and drinking something hot would help settle my stomach. The crew continued to reassure us that the ship was safe and had survived worse. That night I tried to get some sleep, but frequent trips to the head to empty my stomach interfered with any attempt to rest. By morning the sea surge had gradually subsided, and cruising to the next port held no further inconvenience. Sea sickness symptoms subsided to a great extent with the help of more Dramamine, though it surely felt good to walk on *terra firma* when we disembarked. We explored the streets of the tropical town of Aracaju and its sandy beaches. In the evening, as had become routine, we accompanied our sailor friends on the tour of bars in the port area. My stomach wasn't quite ready to tolerate any beer or hard liquor, so I settled for a Coke.

With a cargo of sugar cane, the *Penelope* left port the following afternoon. After a two day stay in Vitoria to unload and re-load cargo we continued south through mostly hot weather. On arrival at Porto Alegre, the Brazilian couple had reached home. "Look us up if you ever visit Porto Alegre" they said, passing around their address and phone number. They went ashore with their belongings, followed by the goodbyes and well wishes of the other passengers.

The long voyage with its adventures was drawing to an end. The ship entered Argentinean waters late in the evening, dropping its anchors a mile from the port of Buenos Aires, awaiting orders to be directed to her assigned pier the next morning. From the deck I could see the bright lights of the city welcoming me back home. It was our last night aboard. I sought out Laura to say, "Hasta pronto," a suggestive, "See you soon." I gave her a telephone number where she could reach me.

As the *Penelope,* my home for the past 32 days, slowly glided to her mooring the next morning, I saw family members standing on the pier waving with excitement. My parents, brother and sister, Aunt Julia and Paul, along with my friends Enrique Casanello, Edmundo Spollansky, Ricardo Pezman and Victor Mizraji, formed the welcoming party. I was overwhelmed by feelings of endearment and happiness at being home again, although temporarily.

All passengers were on deck saying their farewells with wishes of good fortune. I had said my goodbyes to the friendly sailors the evening before, knowing the next morning they would be occupied with the tasks of preparing to dock.

I hadn't seen my family or friends for almost two years. Greeting them again, I was somewhat unprepared for the intensity of the conflicting emotions surging through me. I was glad to be back, but knew I had to prepare to leave them once again. I decided to enjoy my stay while it lasted, putting aside if possible, the emotional conflicts right up until the moment of my departure. Our happy group went together to my parent's place where the conversation centered on my experiences in the United States and the boat trip. I purposely omitted any discussion of future plans. There would be time to discuss and debate them privately. My mother prepared a welcoming meal we all enjoyed. The following weeks were busy ones with long conversations. I divided my time visiting with friends and relatives.

I met Enrique at the clinic and had a tour of the facility. "I'm afraid there won't be any openings in the near future," Enrique mentioned with a sad expression. Smiling, I replied, "Don't worry. Let me give you an update of my own plans." I then told Enrique of my wedding plans and intention to pursue psychiatry as my future specialty. "I could see patients on a short-term basis while I am here, either psychiatric or surgical cases. It would certainly help my finances," I continued. Without hesitation, Enrique offered the use of his private office.

"I'll spread the word that you'll be available to see patients in my office. Being trained in the U.S. will attract some patients," encouraged Enrique. The very next day I placed an advertisement in the *Buenos Aires Herald*, a newspaper printed in English, offering "Short term treatment by a United States trained psychiatrist." Friends in the medical community also came to the rescue by referring cases requiring minor surgery or requesting psychiatric consultations. Enrique had arranged for the clinic's facilities to be available to me. In the six weeks of my stay, I was able to treat enough patients to return to Gardner with substantial money in my pocket.

I had a number of conversations with my parents, discussing the upcoming wedding and my plans for living abroad in the future. They were pleased with Dolores's appearance in the photograph, but they didn't know her or her family, except from my obviously biased accounts. They were distraught about my intention to live permanently in the United States, despite my reassurance that we could make frequent trips to Buenos Aires. Eventually, they reluctantly acknowledged I was mature enough to know my own mind and philosophically acquiesced to my plans.

A week into my stay, I received a phone call from Laura. I wasn't surprised. We arranged to meet the next day at 6:00 p.m. in a downtown *Confiteria*, a bar/tearoom style of place. During this encounter we had a lively, highly seductive interlude ending with an agreement to meet again. I wasted no time contacting Enrique to use his apartment for our *rendezvous*.

"In the boat coming down I met a woman with whom I had a meeting this evening, and we want to spend a few hours together," I explained.

"Thursday will be a good day," said Enrique, "I'll be at the clinic all afternoon. Come at noon to get the key."

That first tryst was one of the several we had before I returned to the United States. We began with full understanding that this would be a short interlude, which was acceptable to both.

Guilt was an emotion I felt infrequently. I was governed by a cultural structure I acknowledged philosophically, and to which I adhered as a course of honor. Having a sexual liaison while engaged to be married was not contrary to my culture as I understood it. Such behavior was a male prerogative to which I felt entitled.

When I had departed for the United States just over two years ago, it was for a predetermined period of time. Now, I was leaving my family, friends, and my country; most probably for the rest of my life. I was overwhelmed by feelings of guilt and betrayal so pervasive that I unconsciously had repressed them deep in the recesses of my mind. Choosing to live distant from my natal family conflicted with my sense of filial duty, however, I envisioned a life of happiness with my future wife.

I purchased a ticket on L.A.N., the Chilean airline, to fly back via Miami, and arrived in Boston late in the morning of Saturday, March 8th. Dolores agreed to be at Logan Airport to meet me so we could ride together back to Gardner.

This time, I knew with certainty that my future belonged in the United States, now my adopted country.

CHAPTER EIGHT

Walking from the gate into the waiting area after leaving the plane at Logan Airport, I scanned the small crowd and searched for Dolores. I soon spotted her. She flashed a brilliant smile as soon as I caught her eye, her face radiating happiness. Our embrace lasted a long while with both whispering in unison in the others ear, "I love you."

On the ride back, Dolores wanted to learn about my parents' reactions, comments from friends and relatives, and experiences about the trip. "Hold it, hold it!" I broke in, "We have plenty of time to talk about it. Tell me about you. Did you miss me?"

"What a silly question!" she shot back, reaching over to kiss me. "Hey, watch out! Watch your driving!" I cautioned.

We drove directly to her parents' house where I was received with great joy and excitement. The entire family had gathered to greet me. I was very appreciative of the warm reception, but I really just wanted to spend time alone with Dolores.

That evening and most of the day Sunday, Dolores flooded me with details of the wedding preparations. I had bought a gold bracelet for her in Buenos Aires that had bankrupted the *Back to Argentina Fund*. I surprised her with it and felt within her happiness that I had returned home, a confusing concept coming on the heels of the empty feelings of leaving home I had experienced when I departed from Buenos Aires. I tried to integrate the conflicting turmoil with the concept that now I would have two homes.

Monday was the first day back to work. I walked from the Mansion to Thompson Hall and was received with friendly greetings and welcoming smiles. At the end of the hall I spotted Grazina who practically ran to greet me. Disregarding professional behavior she threw her arms around me in a motherly hug and blurted, "I knew you'd come back!"

Caught by surprise, it took me a few seconds to react. "What do you mean? Did people think I wasn't coming back?"

"Let's go to your office, Dr. DeNapoli." she said softly, regaining her composure. We walked into the office, and she closed the door behind us. She waited until I had sat down before taking her own seat. Was it a gesture of respect, or was this just the way she would act when explaining the obvious to one of her sons?

"Tell me. What's going on?"

Grazina hesitated, and then let her story unfold. "When the word got out that you had proposed, followed by the news of your trip to Argentina, rumors started circulating around that you weren't coming back, and that wanting to tell your parents personally was just an excuse for making your escape." "He was just playing with her." "He had no intention of getting married." "He got cold feet."

"These were comments that swarmed through our community." she said.

I listened gravely. When she took a breath, a wide grin overspread my face. "I guess I fooled a lot of folks!" I chuckled.

"Not me!" replied Grazina; the twinkle in her eyes brightened her expression of obvious relief.

Reflecting alone in the office, I tried to imagine how disheartening and difficult it must have been for Dolores. Hopefully she knew my love was deep and sensed my strong desire to marry her. I wanted her to be my wife. I missed her when I was away, and I missed the warmth of our relationship. Dolores hadn't mentioned the rumors, and I wondered if she was waiting for the right time. Mention of those rumors, in fact, didn't surface for some time.

The following weeks were quite busy with the Church's required pre-marital counseling, visits to the photographer, work on the guest list, tuxedo fittings, plans for the honeymoon, and a host of other details. Most of the actual plans fell to Dolores and her mother, but the issues Dolores shared with me were overwhelming. It meant that each eventuality be thought of in advance and addressed.

I asked my friend and colleague Augusto Felix in New York to be my best man. Augusto readily agreed with effusive congratulations.

Dolores and her whole family were saddened by the impossibility of my parents and other family members attending the wedding. Dolores knew of their limited financial resources, and the situation was accepted without comment or conversation, but with empathy.

Dolores's bridal shower was organized by her maid of honor, her first cousin, as was the custom. I spent a weekend in New York celebrating a bachelor's party with friends and saying farewell to my single life.

On the morning of April 26, 1958, the wedding day, Augusto and I dressed in our tuxedos and, tails flapping behind us, went for breakfast at a local diner. We were received with kind-hearted applause when the clientele discovered I was to be married later the same morning. The diner's owner said breakfast was on her for this auspicious occasion.

We were married in a Catholic ceremony replete with all the pomp and formality any bride could want. The organ music reverberated off the barrel vault of the ceiling as the bride walked gracefully down the long aisle to the altar where we said our vows. I missed the presence of my parents but embraced Dolores's family as my own.

Following the wedding reception in the function hall of a distinguished local hotel, we left for our honeymoon in Niagara Falls. We drove away in the old 1954 Pontiac to the cheers and well-wishes of the attendants, parents, and happy guests.

We spent one week at the falls and the next ten days traveling to Toronto, Ottawa, and Montreal, re-entering U.S. territory at Derby Line in Vermont.

As we pulled into the re-entry line, I watched what the cars in front did. This was a ploy I had used since arriving in a country where I was not familiar with its practices. I learned as many processes as possible by paying close attention. As we waited, I watched and hoped to simply replicate what those in front had done. If I didn't understand everything, experience had proved it didn't matter in moving through the line. I was behind six or seven automobiles. In this case, I observed the immigration officer questioning the drivers, checking their credentials, and then signaling them to drive on through.

When I approached the check-point, the officer politely asked Dolores for her place of birth and examined my green card. Then he said something I failed to understand. Assuming that the officer had indicated we could move on, as he had with the other drivers, I pulled ahead, intending to drive away. Before I had gotten very far, a state police cruiser, with lights flashing and siren blaring cut in front of my car, forcing me to stop. The officer approached the side of our car, his hand on his weapon, and sternly ordered me to drive back to the checkpoint.

Dolores was asked to sit in a small waiting area while I was ushered into another office. The officer politely, but firmly, interrogated me and questioned my actions. I tried to justify them as being language based. As it turns out, the check point officer had asked me to, "Please open the trunk." In the meantime, other officers searched our car thoroughly.

I informed the officer that my bride and I were returning from our honeymoon, and that I was employed as a physician at the Gardner State Hospital in Massachusetts. This was confirmed by a phone call to Dr. Cordes. We were then allowed entry and continued the trip with a quasi-apology and a three-hour delay. It was a rather uncomfortable incident, but we laughed about the whole scene periodically all the way home. It was mid-afternoon when we arrived.

Our new address was a spacious house on Neighborhood Road. It was both fun and gratifying to move into our new quarters as a married couple. As we unpacked, we realized that we had spent all our money and my paycheck wasn't due until Friday.

"I think it would be a good idea for you to ask your mother to invite us to dinner," was my suggestion. After returning from Dolores's parents that evening, having borrowed money for groceries, we settled into married life. The feeling of being assimilated into American life and its culture was progressively evolving. I knew that I was entering a new stage of my life.

Life at home was rewarding. Our house on Neighborhood Road became the social center for a group of young relatives and friends attracted by our hospitality, and perhaps the brand-new color TV with built in radio and record player. We celebrated all kind of occasions: birthdays, anniversaries, graduations, holidays, mini-dances, and the usual "for no reason" parties. We watched sporting and civic events in color and played board games with the family. Friday poker nights for pennies became a highly attended institution. On frequent weekend trips to New York City we connected with friends, attended the theater, or listened to jazz sessions with Gene Krupa at the Metropole Café. To satisfy our desire for excitement and adventure, we visited nearby localities, including Providence, Rhode Island, where two physician friends from the Fernandez Hospital resided, which brought great delight to our lives.

During one of our escapades in New York, I took Dolores to Harlem Hospital so she could see where my American experience had begun. Leaving the car in the hotel parking lot, we rode the IRT subway line to upper Manhattan. Visiting Harlem was a new experience for Dolores who was very apprehensive, holding tightly to my arm. Once at the hospital, walking the halls and visiting the medical wards, her anxious feelings escalated. She couldn't comprehend that such a poorly hygienic site functioned as a health facility. Entering the feverish activity of the emergency room heightened her fears to the extreme, and she pleaded for us to leave the hospital at once. On the taxi ride back to the hotel she sighed with relief. I also felt relieved of my concern about bumping into Sylvia during our tour.

The morning of September 26, 1959 dawned as one of the most joyful of our lives as we welcomed the birth of our first child, a boy we named Jorge Spencer. He came to life at 7:52 a.m. at Henry Heywood Hospital in Gardner. My self-perception underwent a radical change for I was now the head of a family.

It was time to take concrete steps toward the goal of becoming a full-fledged member of the psychiatric profession.

With the introduction of psychotropic drugs, treatment programs for mental illness resulted in more rewarding outcomes. Patients considered to be suffering from chronic conditions who had been institutionalized for years responded well to the new generation of psychiatric medications. Many became more manageable and a significant number improved enough to be discharged to home or group-home facilities. I was very enthusiastic about being a contributing member during this breakthrough era of psycho-pharmacology. I wrote scientific papers about particular cases, participated in research studies, and most importantly, fell in love with psychiatry. I made the commitment to dedicate all my efforts to become a board certified psychiatrist.

I was not one to have hung onto the dream of becoming a surgeon, or to any bitterness at having to abandon it either; but finding a new challenge to learn, excel at, and contribute to in a field I valued bestowed the gifts of gratitude and fulfillment.

The first requirements were to engage in a three-year program of approved residency training, and, in time, to obtain a full medical license to practice medicine. My temporary license in Massachusetts was valid for five years and almost two and a half had already elapsed.

Two months earlier, a physician had stopped at the hospital administration office to interview with Dr. Cordes about the possibility of securing a position at Gardner State. When he mentioned being originally from Argentina, Dr. Cordes immediately called me in so we could meet. A position was available because the medical director had retired only two weeks before, and one of the psychiatrists on the staff was to fill that position.

The applicant, Dr. Anibal Herrera, had completed his internship at the Samaritan Hospital in Providence, Rhode Island,

and was friends with the Argentinean physicians from the Fernandez Hospital in Buenos Aires. Once Dr. Herrera had fulfilled the necessary requirements, he was accepted to the medical staff.

He and his wife Gilda moved into my old apartment at the Mansion. Anibal and Gilda quickly became active members in the Neighborhood Road social circle. Within the next two years, Anibal would become instrumental in helping me to achieve one of my goals.

I had written to my father for help in obtaining transcripts of my secondary education and medical school records. I also had a preliminary interview with the clerk supervisor in the Boston office of the Board of Registration in Medicine, who provided me with information regarding the entire necessary requirement for an unrestricted medical license application. The package included the format of the written examination that comprised thirty-five subjects, practically the entire medical curriculum.

Time is of concern only to those who are waiting. Two months later, I received the transcripts, and it took another three weeks before they were translated into English at the language department of Clark University in Worcester. The notarization process involved another week. I submitted the documents with the proper application and filing fee to the board of registration. Then there was nothing to do but wait. Really, there was a lot to be done. At this stage of the process, I scheduled specific periods of time in my busy professional and social schedule to begin studying for the examination. At the same time, I began searching for an approved residency program. I researched psychiatric journals and made phone calls to a number of psychiatric centers. I did this with complete secrecy, except for Grazina, who had been of extreme help in writing letters and making telephone inquiries. I didn't want to jeopardize my position as a member of the medical staff.

The snows of winter were melting away when I finally received a letter from the Board of Registration in Medicine. I excitedly opened it, but after reading the first paragraph, my face fell and Dolores knew the response was negative. The letter read in part, "We regret to inform you that the Board is unable to consider your application as your credentials do not contain a *Diploma of Completion of the High School Curriculum*, as required by the regulations."

I was outraged. I had no doubt that my years of education were on a par with the standards of the U.S. The next morning, I placed a call to the Board's office requesting an appointment with the secretary. A week later I traveled to Boston for the meeting. In my conversation with the Secretary, Dr. David W. Wallwork, I compared my educational background to the *European System of Primary, Secondary and University* curriculum, covering the same number of study years as the *American Educational System*. The secretary was gracious and understanding of my dilemma, but adamant in his interpretation of the regulations.

"What do I have to do in order to qualify?" was my question.

"Well, you may take the G.E.D. exam, which would be acceptable to the Board." replied the secretary. I had absolutely no knowledge of the G.E.D. program. The Secretary proceeded to explain. "The General Education Development exam is an equivalency test for those who have failed to complete a high school education. Consult with the high school principal in your town and he'll be able to guide you through the process." he advised, ending the interview.

I wasted no time. Upon returning home, I immediately made arrangements for a visit to Mr. John Gearan, the principal at Gardner High School. Mr. Gearan was amazed and mystified by the secretary's narrow interpretation of Board regulations. His advice was to apply to the Board of Education in Boston for admission to the G.E.D. examination, recommending the Barron's textbooks for reading material in the subjects required by the test. I promptly filed an application with the Department of Education and purchased the books in social and natural sciences, mathematics, and literature, and began to review them. I reluctantly set aside the medical books until I could circumvent this unexpected obstacle.

Within a three-month period, I had studied, taken the G.E.D. exam, and received the certificate with high passing grades. I mailed the certificate to the Board of Registration, and now had to wait again. Six weeks passed before I received another mailing from the Board. This time I was not concerned since I had complied with all the necessary requirements. I was confident that the letter asserted my acceptance and included the date of the examination. Unfortunately, that was not the case. Once again, the letter stated, "We regret to inform you…. The Board has no proof of your adequate written and oral command of the English language."

I could hardly contain my anger. Why were they making it so difficult? I made yet another call to the Board office and arranged for another meeting with Dr. David W. Wallwork.

"I'm sorry Dr. DeNapoli. The regulations require graduates from foreign medical schools to present proof of proficiency in the English language," professed Dr. Wallwork.

"Dr. Wallwork, haven't we been communicating in English?" I inquired sarcastically.

"I know, I know, but we need a written document for our files." said the secretary. "The high school principal should be able to test your language skills and certify your ability to read, write, and converse in our language."

In the *Jacula Prudentum*, published in 1651 by the Welsh poet and orator George Herbert, he wrote, "Every path hath a puddle." Three hundred and nine years later, I had discovered that "*my* path hath more puddles" than all the potholes in the state of Massachusetts in April.

I had always had a positive outlook on life. Obstacles had never deterred me. But it felt like in this country, I had been secretly enrolled in a track event, the high hurdles, where rules were not revealed to the runners, and were changed periodically by devilish whim. But I would endure. This new puddle would not dampen my resolve.

A telephone call to Mr. Gearan, the local principal, and a detailed explanation of the new problem resulted in Mr. Gearan composing a letter with the required certification.

"Dr. DeNapoli, I'm fully satisfied with your proficiency in the language," he assured me. "Tests are not necessary in your case."

In the autumn of 1960, Dolores and I began making plans to visit Buenos Aires for the first time since our marriage. We would stay for four weeks during April or May of the following year. My parents were delighted. It would be their first opportunity to meet Dolores and their grandson, J. Spencer, who by then would be one and a half years old.

It would be fall in Argentina, a nice time to visit. It had been three years since I had seen my parents, siblings and friends. I was very excited about the trip. Dolores was also happy, though a little apprehensive about meeting her in-laws and other Argentinean relatives, despite the love and joyful anticipation they had expressed for her in their letters.

We needed to make air travel reservations well in advance since there were only two flights weekly from New York to Buenos Aires. We purchased our tickets at the Panagra Airline office in Boston. They would be mailed to us long before the departure date. Dolores had to obtain her passport, which also listed Jorge Spencer, as it was customary to include all children under the age of twelve in their mother's traveling document.

Dolores bought new clothing for herself and for J. Spencer, additional luggage, and gifts for the DeNapoli family. At the hospital, we formally requested our vacation times. All the arrangements were in place, with one exception; the airline tickets had not yet arrived. One afternoon after work, I came home to find Dolores excitedly waving the envelope from the airline.

"We have good news," she practically sang. "I see we got the tickets," I grinned back.

She ran to me, hugged and kissed me, and whispered in my ear "The really good news is that I'm pregnant." Without telling me, that very afternoon, Susan had gone with her to see the doctor who confirmed the suspected and welcomed diagnosis. I couldn't contain my excitement, and yet was unable to express my immense joy in words. She had already shared the good news with her mother, who telephoned shortly to congratulate me.

The good news also brought some concerns. In April, Dolores would be almost five months into her pregnancy. The flight would take about 30 hours, with several landings for refueling, which would require passengers to disembark and re-board at each stop. Worried, we consulted with her doctor, but he reassured us that Dolores was young and in good health, and he could see no reason to anticipate problems with the demands of travel. I knew also that competent medical care would be readily available in Buenos Aires, if the need arose.

The flight was rather uncomfortable for Dolores. The physical stress of flying long hours, frequent landings and take-offs, and lack of adequate sleeping time, tested her strength. J.Spencer, on the contrary, had a great time being catered to by the flight attendants who brought him to the cockpit frequently to be entertained by the pilots. He was amazed by the impressive instrument panel and the vast view of the starry sky at night.

The spectacular panorama of crossing the Andes Mountain Range after leaving the last stop in Santiago, Chile, was breathtaking. The plane appeared to float, suspended only a few feet above the mountain tops. The sunshine on the snow covered peaks, the bottomless wide crevices, and the green patches of the valleys below created a majestic picture of Mother Nature's work. The propeller driven DC-8 craft finally landed to Dolores's relief. Her first long-distance trip was over, and she had managed it well.

A gathering of family members awaited us in the airport lobby. Dolores and J. Spencer immediately became the center of attention, receiving countless expressions of love and affection, while I proudly watched from the sidelines. The reception party continued at my parent's apartment with homemade hors d'oeuvres and plenty of beverages.

Since the apartment had limited living space, it was decided that J. Spencer would stay with his grandparents while Dolores and I lodged in a nearby hotel.

Dolores wholeheartedly enjoyed the entire vacation, including city tours, performances at the Opera House, and entertainment shows at various nightclubs. House parties at relatives and friends made her feel at home. Meeting and bonding with Enrique, Ricardo, Edmundo, Victor and other friends added to her pleasure. Her main difficulty was communicating because of her minimal fluency in Spanish. However, as she was fluent in French, she managed short conversations with those who could speak basic French or some English. I assumed the role of official translator. My parents, siblings, and friends were captivated by Dolores' charming and engaging personality, making every possible effort to make her feel at home. Jorge Spencer enchanted everybody's heart, fully enjoyed his stay, and was, of course, totally spoiled by his grandparents.

On the flight back, Dolores expressed her gratitude at being so lovingly welcomed into her new family. She vowed earnestly to become fluent in Spanish, a pledge she fulfilled by enrolling in a community college course and later by pursuing further studies while we lived in New York.

Back in Gardner, I resumed my routine work schedule, and soon after was offered the position of Clinical Director. I had a candid discussion with Dr. Cordes, graciously declining the offer while explaining my search for an approved residency program as a necessary, formal step to becoming board certified in psychiatry. Dr. Cordes was understanding, offering his full support in helping to achieve my goal.

Dolores had requested a leave-of-absence to dedicate her time to the care of J. Spencer. She fully enjoyed her role as a mother and was pleased her second pregnancy was progressing well.

Unexpectedly one day she discovered slight bleeding accompanied by mild cramps. A prompt consultation with her gynecologist disclosed that premature labor had begun. I rushed her to the Henry Heywood Hospital in Gardner, and she was immediately admitted to the maternity unit. After a short labor, on June 21st 1961 at 2:48 a.m. she gave birth to a premature but healthy baby boy. As we had previously agreed, his first name would be Jorge. His middle name was more difficult to choose.

My preference was Randall, but Dolores and her family objected because the name would not be acceptable to the Catholic Church. Other names were considered; finally arriving at the decision to name him Jorge Alan.

However, the name ended up being for legal purposes only since his almost two-year-old brother, unable to pronounce his given name, started calling him *Tiki* from the very beginning. Ever since, and to this day, everyone has called him by his nickname; very few are aware of his real name.

I applied and was offered a position in the first-year residency program in psychiatry at Concord State Hospital in Concord, New Hampshire. I had visited the city and had been impressed by its New England charm and the friendliness of its people. The teaching medical staff at the hospital was known for its skill and well-organized program, providing ample learning opportunities for their participants.

During one of several interviews with the Director of Clinical Education, I was informed that the program had been certified for only the first year of residency, but that an application had been filed with the Board of Psychiatric Education, Washington D.C., requesting certification for recognized second and third year residencies. The teaching curriculum was in the process of program evaluation, and the hospital expected to be certified in the very near future.

Dolores had accompanied me on one of the visits and had been thrilled with the city, the hospital, and the housing accommodations, which were located right on the well landscaped campus. The larger city of Manchester was only 20 minutes away and Gardner was a relatively short drive of an hour and a half. The financial compensation was slightly more than at

Gardner State. Together, we agreed it was a good opportunity for me to initiate my psychiatric career. I mailed a letter of acceptance, with a starting date of December 5, 1961. We would miss our friends in Gardner, but we were within driving distance, and besides, we would certainly make new friends in our new surroundings.

Shortly after our third wedding anniversary, I filed a citizen application form with the Citizenship and Immigration Services. In order to fulfill the eligibility requirements, I had presented birth and marriage certificates, my permanent resident card, and photos. I had attended interviews for background checks and had been fingerprinted and tested in United States history and civics as required. Two of my American friends had appeared as witnesses certifying that I had no communist affiliations or inclinations. Months later I received a letter of approval with the date of the ceremony to be administered the Oath of Allegiance. December 7th 1961, marked a significant milestone in my life. On that unforgettable morning, before a judge of the Superior Court of Worcester, in the Commonwealth of Massachusetts, I was sworn in as a Citizen of the United States of America and awarded a Certificate of Naturalization. Reciting the Pledge of Allegiance was one of my proudest moments since I had stepped on American soil at the Miami Airport that sunny February morning in 1956. Dolores, with J. Alan in her arms and J. Spencer standing by her side, along with relatives and friends, had been present to witness this memorable event, sharing the joy and pride-filled solemnity.

Our new living quarters was the first-floor apartment in a house with a similar vacant unit upstairs. Soon after the New Year, a young German couple moved in upstairs. Kristof and

Monika Herrmann, originally from Munich, had moved from Union City, New Jersey, where he had completed his internship. He was also starting the first year of his residency. We soon became good friends, and when Dolores learned that Monika was four months pregnant, she was quite helpful in guiding her path to motherhood. When Melanie-Therese was born, Dolores and I were asked to be the godparents, by proxy, for relatives in Germany. As close friends, we traveled together to different locations in New England, meeting friends and relatives in Gardner. Kristof was an avid reader of World History and we had frequent animated discussions since I was also fond of the subject.

Because Monika was attentive to Melanie Therese to the level of overprotection, I nicknamed her "Mother Hen," a familiarity I continued to employ for years. A surprising revelation during our first visit to Munich several years later to reconnect with our German friends changed my perception, making it seem somehow inappropriate to continue calling her by that nickname.

As a child, Monika had witnessed the horrors of World War II, particularly the Allied bombing of her home town of Munich. As a consequence, she was overly sensitive to loud, explosive-like noises, usually reacting with sudden fright. Severe thunderstorms were common in the Concord area and they would bring back memories of her childhood during the war. When they occurred, Mother Hen would run downstairs with Melanie-Therese in her arms seeking reassurance and comfort from Dolores and me.

I gained vast satisfaction and valuable experience in this new teaching environment. The learning came more easily to me than to my fellow residents because of the years at Gardner State Hospital. My management of complicated cases earned me the positions of Training Supervisor and Assistant to the Educational Director.

A source of increasing concern was the realization that the approval of the second- and third-year residency program had not been forthcoming. My concern was vaporized by a phone call from Anibal Herrera who had left Gardner for a three-year residency program at Middletown Psychiatric Center in Middletown, New York. The program was affiliated with the Psychiatric Institute at Columbia University in New York City.

At Anibal's insistence, I visited him, learning that there were seven open positions in the program at Columbia, with residents assigned to Middletown Psychiatric Center for in-field training. The Center would afford housing and a monthly stipend, although lower than my present salary. The Center's offer held the excellent possibility of resolving my dilemma. The inconvenient part would be the daily commute to the Psychiatric Institute in New York City. *Not a big problem,* I surmised. The commute was only an hour and fifteen minutes in a carpool with other residents.

The two stumbling blocks were the requirements of having a medical license in any of the states and passing the entrance examination.

Returning to Concord, and with great excitement, I gave Dolores an account of this golden opportunity. It would be to my professional advantage to complete the training at Columbia University. Living close to New York City would be an added benefit.

I hadn't heard from the Board of Registration in Massachusetts. Contacting them resulted in a reply letter with the information that my credentials were still in the process of being evaluated.

On an off-duty afternoon, I walked the four blocks to the municipal building where the New Hampshire Board of Registration in Medicine was located. While talking to the receptionist regarding the application process and the necessary requirements, the office door labeled, Edward W. Colby, MD, Secretary of the Board, opened. The receptionist promptly introduced me. "Dr. DeNapoli is requesting information regarding licensure."

"Dr. DeNapoli, please come in," said Dr. Colby, signaling toward his office. I had brought photocopies of all my credentials in anticipation of filing an application and submitting the documentation.

"Please sit down. Let me review those documents," requested the secretary. As he was viewing them one-by-one, he came across the G.E.D. certificate. In an inquisitive manner he asked, "Why did you take the G.E.D. exam?" I explained the rigorous requirements of the Massachusetts Board. Dr. Colby raised his eyebrows, shook his head in disbelief and assured me, "You will not need this here," and handed the certificate back to me.

"Leave your credentials and the application with the receptionist. We'll review them at the Board Meeting next week. The next examination for licensure is scheduled for March 17th, explained Dr. Colby.

Walking back to the hospital, I was amazed at the cordiality of the interview, and the simplicity of the process compared to Massachusetts.

Up to the time we had moved to New Hampshire, I had been reviewing various medical subjects in anticipation of the Massachusetts licensure test. I felt well prepared, with just the need for a quick review before appearing for the New Hampshire examination in three weeks. It was an unforgettable moment; the day I received a certified letter of notification that I had successfully passed the qualifying test, granting me an unrestricted license to practice medicine in the State of New Hampshire. My eyes were teary when I broke the happy news to Dolores. I had completed another chapter of my master plan.

On Saturday night Dolores organized a celebration party, inviting our upstairs neighbors and in-town friends, among other friends and relatives from Gardner. My trusted secretary Grazina was also a welcome guest.

With Anibal's assistance, I had completed the necessary documentation to register for the entrance exam for the Columbia University Psychiatric Institute. In late September, we, and approximately 200 other applicants, took the test. Anibal and I thought that being accepted into one of the seven available positions was likely as our years of psychiatric experience at Gardner gave us an advantage over the other candidates. Our hunch proved to be correct. We received letters of acceptance to enroll for courses in the second- and third-year residency program, commencing on December 3rd, 1962.

Life in Concord continued to be professionally and socially rewarding. I progressively increased my psychiatric experience and knowledge, becoming more confident in managing complex situations in the psychiatric field. Our sons were growing up healthy and Dolores was happy in her role as mother and wife.

The cold gusts of early November winds swirled multicolored leaves when we began preparations for the move to New York. I anxiously anticipated joining the Ivy League atmosphere of Columbia University, ready to meet the demanding expectations of their residency program.

In the interim, Kristof had secured a position at the Neuropsychiatric Institute at Princeton University in New Jersey, on the recommendation of a German family friend, a professor in the language department. He would start in mid-January. This was good news because they would be just a two-hour drive from Middletown. We could visit often or meet halfway in New York City, continuing our close friendship.

CHAPTER NINE

On the first weekend of that December, we moved into our furnished apartment on the grounds of Middletown State Hospital, across the street from Anibal and Gilda. The next two years were a swirl of activity. Progress toward my professional goals brought great satisfaction. Dedication to my work, and successes in treating complex cases earned an assignment to the Vanderbilt Clinic at Columbia-Presbyterian Hospital where I supervised students in a six-month psychotherapy course.

I periodically thought about Doctor Bradford Peterson who worked on the surgical floor above. The residue of our previous meeting, as well as the irony of our proximity, led me to fantasize about an encounter that would prove to Dr. Peterson that I would have been an asset to the surgical department. I revisited the experience, observing the man I had been back then as he felt rejected and dealt with the reality that my skill wasn't enough to create a place for me. The fantasy helped complete the process of letting go of the frustration and anger that the interview with him had kindled. I think my psychiatric training helped this process of realizing how completely I had moved on and the satisfaction of being of the professional I had become.

This new-found peace of mind was facilitated by my contentment. I was happy in my marriage and took great delight in my children. It might have deepened my compassion and patience to consider how different my story might have been if there had truly been no way out. But it is a quantum leap from accommodating the brush-off of a colleague one wished to be mentored by to being able to generalize about the dark places where some of our mental instabilities germinate.

The local health facility in Middletown, Horton Memorial Hospital, advertised their need for a physician's team to manage the emergency room, overnight, Monday through Friday, and 24-hours a day Saturday and Sunday. Anibal, Akim, (a Turkish psychiatric resident in the hospital) and I decided to apply for the position as a means of supplementing our incomes. Despite the love for and successes in psychiatry, I had always found the opportunity to treat medical and surgical patients appealing. We had an interview with Horton's Executive Board and were awarded the contract. The number of patients seeking care on weeknights was minimal, and only one physician had to be in attendance, permitting us to rotate our schedules. Working only two or three nights per week, we still could get enough sleep to function in our other capacities. On weekends we rotated through 12-hour shifts, and, as the number of patients seeking emergency treatment was substantial, we welcomed Alice Krump, MD, a newly established general practitioner in town, who was eager to participate in the rotation. I was pleased by the chance to update my knowledge of medical and surgical procedures. My previous experiences in Buenos Aires and in the Emergency Room at Harlem Hospital more than qualified me.

Our team was proud of our work, which also allowed us to expand our social activities as a result of the extra discretionary income. All was well until a tragic event disrupted the tranquility of our social lives and dimmed the glow of recent achievements.

Alessandro Musa and his wife Lucia had lived for the past two years on the opposite side of the street from our apartment. Alessandro was originally from Italy, while his wife, ten years his junior, had been born on Long Island. They had no children. Alessandro was a jovial, outgoing man and respected psychiatrist, and well-liked by the hospital community. Living in such close proximity, we had developed a friendly relationship with him. Alessandro was a master at the game of chess. Early almost every evening, he and I would schedule an hour for play. The game might last for weeks. Anibal and Akim would join in special chess tournaments with our wives organizing house parties that included the children. Since Alessandro's place had a back yard, it was the designated location for summer BBQs.

One Saturday during an early winter evening in January, Dolores answered a frantic phone call from Lucia. Alessandro was complaining of severe chest pains. Lucia was terrified. Dolores screamed for me as I was playing with the boys on the porch. Racing across the street, I found Alessandro on the couch gasping for air. His face was ashen, drops of cold sweat beaded his forehead, and his hands grasped at his chest. His lips were already blue and his pulse was faint and irregular. The diagnosis was unquestionable and alarming; Alessandro was having a heart attack.

I grabbed the phone and called the hospital requesting an ambulance, asking the operator to alert the ER staff that a possible heart attack patient would be arriving in minutes. I also called Akim, whom I knew was at home, to help. Akim came immediately and together we did all we could to make Alessandro comfortable until the ambulance arrived. It took ten minutes, seemingly an eternity, watching our friend's life slipping away. I accompanied Alessandro in the ambulance. Half way to the hospital, he lost consciousness and stopped breathing. I began CPR and artificial breathing. As the stretcher carrying Alessandro was wheeled into the Emergency Room, Anibal, who was on duty at the time, was ready with an injection of intra-cardiac adrenaline. An anesthetist, who happened to be at the hospital, was ready with a portable breathing apparatus to intubate him. We were all aware that Alessandro had technically expired but made every effort to revive him. We frantically worked for more than forty minutes with no sign of life, unwilling to accept that further efforts were futile. Ultimately, we had to abandon our friend to his death. We embraced with tears streaming down our faces. No words could express our feelings of impotence and loss. Our friend was gone.

Dolores and Gilda accompanied Lucia to the hospital. The women read the devastating news by our body language before our words confirmed it. I hugged Lucia tightly while she sobbed inconsolably on my shoulder.

Funeral services were held in Mineola, Long Island, Lucia's hometown where she returned to live with relatives.

Alessandro's death was the most personally painful tragedy I had ever experienced. He appeared to be in good health. He was a loving and generous man. He was a slightly older, but a vibrant edition of our lives. Not only had an acute disease snatched him away, but we, his friends, fellow physicians, had been unable to intervene successfully. It was sobering. His passing somewhat dimmed the brightness of my life but reinforced my emotional commitment to family and friends.

Alessandro died on January 11, 1964. He was only forty-five years old.

Dolores and I were grateful to have Kristof and his wife relatively close by. We visited frequently, either in Princeton, Middletown, or New York City where we attended the theater, movies, art shows, children activities, or dined at our favorite restaurants. Unfortunately, we would soon lose this close relationship, when Kristof and Monika decided to return to their native Munich. Kristof had completed his residency and was offered an assistant professorship at a psychiatric center affiliated with the *Ludwig-Maximilian-Universitat-Munchen*. The appointment was prestigious and well paid; obviously too tempting an offer to refuse.

Because of Monika's fear of flying, especially with almost three-year old Melanie- Therese, they decided to cruise to Hamburg and then travel by train to Munich. Due to their imminent departure, we drove down from Georgetown, Massachusetts, where we had recently relocated after completing my training in New York. We spent two nights together in the city before bidding each other farewell. Standing on the Maritime Company pier was an emotional time for everyone, especially for Monika and me.

Over the past two years we had allowed our relationship to cross the boundaries of friendship. It had begun innocently enough, but our close friendship developed into physical attraction that was at first only noticed unconsciously, but then subtly communicated by nuance of body language and the telepathic certainty of one another desires. These circumstances would not necessarily have been apparent to the casual observer; and possibly we may have remained simply very close friends except for a chance encounter at Luchow's, a German restaurant on 14th Street in Manhattan, frequented by the four of us when together in the city.

One day after completing assignments at the Psychiatric Institute in late morning, I decided to have a light lunch at Luchow's. I was surprised to see Monika sitting at the other end of the long bar. We greeted each other with a hug as usual, but it was unexpectedly much tighter than customary. Was this really pure coincidence? Our meeting *wasn't* planned. Monika had spent the morning shopping and innocently stopped for lunch. As we ate together, without explanation or mutual design, suddenly all barriers dissolved and lust consumed us both. A room in a nearby hotel witnessed the fervor of our repressed attraction; our lovemaking ardent and compelling. Afterward, we both felt the guilt of betraying spouses and mutual friends. We were aware of the power of our feelings which could delight or destroy. Ours was not an encounter born of boredom or repressed anger towards our partners in marriage. It was a mixture of real love imbued with the ever-present lust of vibrant human beings. Swans mate for life. The biology of that is poignant, especially after the death of one of them, but what of humans? There was no equivocating or intellectualizing our afternoon's tryst. We had, like moths, flown near to a flame that could consume our happiness, our spouses and our children. We agreed this would be a singular event, and it was a promise we did not break. At the pier on that morning of Monika's leaving, our eyes affirmed our love for one another, conveyed the poignancy of parting, and acknowledged that our secret would remain ours alone.

Bad news may come in bunches, but good news can also be clustered together in sweet bouquets. Dolores discovered she was pregnant with our third child, with the due date at the end of May. I received word of a promotion, implying a pay raise. And in the autumn of 1963, I had finally been notified by the licensure board in Massachusetts that my credentials had been accepted and I was eligible to take the examination scheduled for February of the following year. When I took stock of my life, it was very full. The responsibility of raising two boys brought joy alongside the awareness of the financial obligations, the professional requirements of the residency training program, and the commitment to my emergency room practice. Now I needed to find time to study for the upcoming licensing exam, plus I had to provide moral support for Dolores during her pregnancy, as well as prepare for the arrival of a new family member. I was confident I could manage everything, even as I felt the weight on my shoulders. I was determined nothing in my path would cause me to stumble, or even to break stride.

Dolores was pregnant with our third child, with a due date in May. Our friend Gilda announced that she was also pregnant for the second time, hoping for a successful delivery in October. This was an occasion for celebration because a diagnosis of eclampsia had resulted in the loss of Gilda's unborn child two years before. A healthy baby girl arrived on October 20th to the joy of her parents. Gilda's widowed mother traveled from Argentina to be by her side and to assist with maternal duties.

For some reason, Gilda never established meaningful relationships in the community. Her social contacts were limited to transient interactions with other Spanish-speaking ladies whose husbands were participants in the psychiatric residency program at the hospital. These relationships usually terminated as the men moved on to further their careers. Dolores repeatedly invited Gilda to join her circle of friends and acquaintances, shop together, come to Dolores's book club, or join the Ladies Auxiliary at the hospital, all to no avail. Gilda repeatedly declined all activities that would facilitate her adaptation into American culture. Instead, she poured all her attention into her new daughter and her close relationship with her mother who remained with them for many months.

As the years passed, Gilda continued to struggle with feelings of loneliness and homesickness as she mourned the life and culture of her native Argentina. Anibal had enthusiastically come to the United States with the intention of pursuing a career in psychiatry, and he wished to reside here permanently. He had, in fact, already applied for U.S. citizenship. I surmised she had been opposed to Anibal's intention of emigrating from the beginning.

Eventually she decided to return to her country with her daughter and live with her mother. Gilda held a Ph.D. in psychology and planned to practice her profession in Buenos Aires. She made no commitments about her future intentions. Anibal was devastated and angry with Gilda's decision. He was depressed and full of rage over his wife's unwillingness to negotiate their future. He spent hours with me trying to work through his feelings of rejection and frustration about being kept apart from his daughter. He viewed Gilda's behavior as stubbornly manipulative. He felt she had essentially hijacked their daughter, giving him the ultimatum, "Live where I want to live, or live without your daughter."

Hoping their situation would change, he continued providing for his absent family by purchasing a comfortable condo in an elegant section of Buenos Aires for their use and sending monthly financial support. Time passed with no change in Gilda's willingness to rejoin Anibal in the States, though she occasionally visited him for short periods of time. Anibal grew increasingly pessimistic and discouraged about his marriage, without totally facing the reality of his wife's strong feelings about not rejoining him in America. And then Laura entered the scene. Laura was a young nurse from the hospital. They began to date and their relationship quickly deepened. Anibal had successfully passed the licensure examination in New York State and was firm in his determination to make Middletown his permanent address. He opened a psychiatric clinic in the downtown area and remained part time at the Middletown Psychiatric Center. Over the years he always maintained a relationship with his daughter, traveling to visit her often, and watching her develop into a mature and beautiful young woman.

With Laura, Anibal had found a love he could truly share, and their relationship has continued to flourish for over four decades.

Some friends complete their journey in life too soon; other relationships fade away due to family commitments or in career pursuits. The wisdom and caprice of the universe fills the void with possibilities of new friendships, reinforcing the thought that we belong to each other in many concrete ways, but for finite lengths of time.

A new family moved into Anibal and Gilda's apartment across the street. Dolores and I took slightly longer to extend ourselves to the newcomers, both because of the sadness of the apartment's former occupants and because the new family was not white. The couple had two children, a boy, Dennis, and his younger sister, Jamille; the joy of their parents.

Dennis and my older son Spencer, being of approximately the same age, promptly developed a close relationship, and were frequently joined in their games by Tiki. Dolores soon became acquainted with Leah while supervising their children at play. In no time they were visiting each other with the children, and spending time in each other's homes. The turning point in both family's relationship was the occasion of our up-coming wedding anniversary one April.

To celebrate, we organized a get-together at our apart-ment, inviting our closest local friends and those relatives will-ing to endure the four-hour-long drive to Middletown, NY. Among the invited guests were the across-the-street new neigh-bors Kendall and Leah Whitton. After one phone call I took in response to our invitation, Dolores asked if I had mentioned the Whittons' race.

`Why should I do that?" I asked. She didn't have an an-swer, but the reality was that someone attending could have been surprised by a bi-racial guest list.

Dolores was not racially prejudiced, but at that time in race-relations the country was embroiled in re-examining atti-tudes and segregation issues. The fabric of American culture concerning the topic was still practically as frayed as it had been since the Civil War, and violence surfaced across a land still reeling from assassination. Many Americans had no more chance to know Afro-Americans than the Argentinean who had been taught *their* liberated slaves traveled to Brazil because the climate was more to their liking.

As it turned out the Whitton's simply ended-up enjoy-ing the anniversary celebration that day with all the other guests. This first formal social occasion cemented a long relationship.

Ken was a graduate of Southern Polytechnic State Uni-versity in Marietta, Georgia, and they had moved north in search of better opportunities in a more receptive social environment.

He had been hired by the hospital as the assistant comp-troller in the finance department. His wife Leah was a certified middle school teacher searching for a position in the local school district.

As our friendship grew, both families shared a closer lifestyle. To the children's delight, we took our mixed group to a nearby lake resort that offered swimming and canoeing. One of our favorite places to visit was West Point, overlooking the Hudson, only an hour's drive away. On special Sundays, we could watch the Corps of Cadets military drills followed by the full dress parade. The children, especially Dennis, were always fascinated by the elegant posture of the cadets marching to the sounds of the military band. Even at that early age, Dennis, just six years old, would repeatedly express his desire to someday enter the military academy. On other occasions, we hired a babysitter so that we could enjoy a night of dining and dancing or theater in New York City.

Ken imparted a substantial amount of business and financial knowledge to me through our frequent conversations. I regretted the one-sided aspect of the transfer of information. I would have liked to be useful to Ken in a reciprocal way. Beyond his position at the hospital, Ken was primarily interested in academia, always alert to any opportunity to enter that field.

After I completed the training at Middletown Psychiatric Center and Columbia University, and moved back to Massachusetts, I learned Ken had secured an assistant professorship in the business department of the University of Rochester in Rochester, NY. Though we no longer lived across the street, our friendship continued for years, with alternating visits between our families.

As my residency program neared completion, I had grown into the role of a confident, rising professional, with Dolores supporting and encouraging me each step of the way. With both my mainsail and rudder, I captained our family into the future of our dreams.

I was still working toward obtaining the elusive license to practice medicine in Massachusetts; a much more difficult task than it seemed it should be. On the weekend of February 8th, 1964, I drove to the state house in Boston to take the licensure test in a conference room at the Board of Registration. I stayed at the Touraine Hotel across the Common, feeling well prepared for the grueling four-and-a-half-day examination.

Six weeks later, I received the long-awaited notification confirming that persistence and hard work had at last paid off. I had passed the test and was finally fully licensed to practice medicine in Massachusetts. We were in a celebratory mood all spring, culminating with the birth of a daughter on May 29th 1964. We named her Deirdre Dolores.

She was born at 6:32 PM at the Horton Memorial Hospital in Middletown, NY.

Dolores, a graduate of the Saint Joseph Hospital School of Nursing in Lowell, Massachusetts, was familiar with the city, and had many friends and classmates in the area. I had liked New England since I had first arrived in Gardner. Our long-range plan had always been to settle somewhere in the North Shore region of the Bay State.

Now that our family was growing, my responsibilities increased substantially as well. To further improve my resume, I had applied for licensure in New York State using the reciprocity provisions of the Massachusetts license. The only added requirement was to successfully pass a test in a limited number of subjects, not a difficult task as I had been reviewing the medical curriculum almost constantly for the past three years.

As autumn approached, I began inquiries to relocate to Massachusetts. Being a newcomer to medical circles in the area, and mindful of the financial responsibilities of a growing family, it seemed unwise, if not impossible, to make a living by opening a private practice. The only alternative was to find a salaried position with a well-established psychiatrist or in a psychiatric unit. I would scout the area, visit general hospitals, and discuss my intentions with Dolores's professional acquaintances from her training days, or solicit referrals from her nurse friends.

Advertisements in psychiatric journals offering possible salaried positions were another source of information. Eventually, I responded to an ad from Baldpate Hospital, a private psychiatric institution located on the outskirts of Georgetown, Massachusetts a short distance from Lowell and only a 45-minute ride from Boston. I was delightfully impressed by the quaint appearance of the hospital and the middle-class residential community.

My interview with the Director, Dr. Patrick Quirke, resulted in an immediate meeting of minds and purpose. Dr. Quirke, who spoke with an unmistakable Irish brogue, was a graduate of the University of Dublin, Trinity College for Health Sciences, and had been in circumstances similar to the ones I had to overcome in my quest to settle in America.

A few days after reviewing my credentials, a phone call from Dr. Quirke approved my appointment to the psychiatric staff. A follow-up letter officially confirmed my employment as Assistant Director with a salary of $18,000.00, almost three times my present earnings, including a rented house in town. The starting date was set as December 5th 1964, coinciding with the completion of my three-year training in New York.

As soon as the family was established in our new residence in Georgetown, Dolores contacted former friends and classmates, quickly resulting in the flowering of our social life. The relative proximity to Gardner also brought closer interaction with Dolores's side of the family and old friends from the area.

I brought to my new professional environment the latest in psychopharmacology treatments, using new drugs and new ideas in therapeutic approaches to a somewhat stagnant psychiatric setting. My vitality and innovations were enthusiastically received by Dr. Quirke and the nursing staff who fully supported all efforts to update the hospital to Ivy League standards. The adjustment was fulfilling. I was proud of the position as Assistant Director, even though Dr. Quirke had failed to mention one minor detail. As we were the only two psychiatrists in the institution, there was no one for me to teach or supervise.

The 46-bed hospital was privately owned by a prominent Boston psychiatrist who was also an administrator in the Department of Mental Health. It provided both in-patient and out-patient psychiatric services to an exclusive clientele, accepted only by referral. Patients came from across the United States as well as countries abroad.

With my own office and a personal secretary, I was able to arrange my own schedule. Hospital regulations allowed me to start a limited private practice, which became thriving and remunerative in less than a year. As I began to be known in the medical community, an invitation to join the medical staff as a consulting psychiatrist at the Hale Hospital, in the neighboring city of Haverhill, was soon forthcoming.

CHAPTER TEN

Given the substantial improvement of our finances, the time had come for us to buy the first home we could actually call our own. We defined our requirements. The new house had to be no further than a 30-minute drive from Baldpate Hospital, in a quiet residential community with a reputable school system, and allow for further expansion of my private practice. With these non-negotiables in mind, Dolores began exploring the surrounding towns and contacting real estate agencies in her search for the home that would meet our family's needs.

She inspected houses for sale and selected those appropriate for us. In the evenings, after work, we would visit them. Eventually, she found one meeting all our requirements; in her opinion, the ideal house. Without divulging her feelings with me, she arranged for a mutual viewing, holding back her own excitement in anticipation of my possible reaction.

Dolores and I pulled into the circular driveway showcasing the stately manor. Upon entering the elegant foyer adorned with wide, wooden crown moulding, we were met by a graciously curved staircase that arched upward and past light slanting through a ceiling-high stained-glass window. We toured the spacious fire-placed living room, the banquet-sized dining room, and the modern kitchen with its Dutch-tiled hearth. The second and third stories opened to four bedrooms, a study, sitting room, and walk-in cedar closet. Bathrooms were everywhere. I had been silent, carefully observing and cataloging each detail as we walked from room to room. Finally, I turned to Dolores with a widely approving smile, exclaiming, "You've found our new home!"

We moved into 16 Hidden Road in the town of Andover, on December 7th, 1965. For months we ate off cardboard boxes, a large sheet also serving as a curtain over the dining room window that opened onto the street's frontage. All other windows were curtainless. It took more than a year to complete the furnishings, step-by-step. We were in love with our homestead. The ten-room home, built in 1915, had the charm of yesteryear, unspoiled by recently remodeled updates to the kitchen and to the five modernized bathrooms.

It was time to implement the dream I had harbored for years: to have my parents visit the United States. I purchased the airline passages and made all the necessary arrangements with the American Embassy in Buenos Aires. On a cool, sunny morning in the spring of 1966, we welcomed my mother and father at JFK International Airport in New York. The effusive expressions of happiness were indescribable. It had been almost five years since we all had been together. The drive to Andover exploded in laughter, wonderment, and expressions of love and affection.

My father staggered with joy upon entering our home. Tears of pride filled his eyes. J. Spencer, Tiki, and Deirdre received them waving small American and Argentinean flags, symbolizing the blending of my roots and the reward of my northern adventure. We were all filled with gratitude for our good fortune and determined to make their stay unforgettable.

My father and I luxuriated in conversing about Argentina detailing disturbing events causing unrest in my native land. These evoked memories long dormant in my mind, making the past seem alive once more.

My youth in Buenos Aires coincided with the regime of Juan Domingo Peron and his wife, Evita. During my years of secondary education, and then as a university student, I had strongly disapproved of the policies of a political system that curtailed civil liberties while at the same time awarding trade unions unlimited power. I spoke up against the government's tyrannical tactics to the point of becoming an activist, organizing student demonstrations. I had frequently been pursued by the much-feared Federal Police, but I always managed to evade detention. My older brother Omar was less fortunate. He and several of his associates were arrested during a political rally and sentenced without a trial to forty days confinement in a military facility.

Our family feared for his fate and physical well-being as torture was commonly used to obtain names and addresses of other followers. Fortunately, he was released at the end of his sentence without having undergone any mistreatment. Later, when drafted into the Army in 1951, I had had no alternative but to participate, when ordered, in repressive operations.

Fortunately, as a member of the Medical Corps, my involvement was limited to providing medical assistance and care.

During those times of student unrest, I happened to cross paths with Ernesto R. Guevara de la Serna, later known as *Che*

Guevara. *Che* is a familiar Argentinean interjection to call attention, and was years later used by Guevara's Latino followers to identify his Argentinean origin. Ernesto, as he was then known, was the son of a well-to-do family with strong leftist leanings. He attended medical school two years ahead of me. He was passionate about spreading his communist views and was frequently seen on campus and street corners distributing Marxist literature. Most university students considered him to be a misinformed misfit. He seldom influenced anyone with his political agenda. Argentina at the time was characterized by a far-right government and a moderate right-wing population with strong religious beliefs; not fertile ground for his leftist rhetoric. I had numerous confrontations with Ernesto, exchanging widely opposing political views: he emphasizing the highlights of his Marxist agenda against my strong conviction in the social benefits of a democratic system.

In 1951, Ernesto put his medical career on hold, and took a year-long motorcycle ride with a friend, searching for a location to use as a base for his Marxist ideology in South and Central American countries. He later detailed his experiences in a book entitled, *The Motorcycle Diaries*. After he completed his medical studies and graduated with a medical degree, he again left the country, eventually meeting Fidel Castro in Mexico in 1954, where he joined Castro's Revolutionary Army.

Under Peron's government, I recalled living through interminable days of mourning, including flags at half mast, black cloth-draped balconies, canceled classes and festive activities, following Evita's death on July 26, 1952, at the age of 33. For days-on-end, a mandatory five-minute period of mourning was ordered in all public institutions and schools.

The only war-like experience I became embroiled in occurred during an attack ordered by dissident officers in June of 1955, in an attempt to overthrow Peron's government. Navy and Air Force aircraft bombarded the government's house, *La Casa*

Rosada, and the ministerial buildings around Plaza de Mayo, the city's central square. This military action killed and wounded numerous civilians and military personnel. The attack was deliberately timed to coincide with people leaving work for their lunch hour from many private and government institutions in the vicinity of Plaza de Mayo.

I lived only a few blocks away and was on my way to work at the Fernandez Hospital. Witnessing the assault, I altered my usual public transportation commute and hailed a taxi. The driver was reluctant to take a fare under the ongoing bombardment, but I identified myself as a medical doctor, explaining the urgency for me to get to the hospital. When I arrived, the hospital's pre-established Disaster Emergency Plan had been activated, and had already organized surgical teams to attend the wounded who were continuously arriving, hastily piled in ambulances.

Assigned to one team, I spent the next 15 hours in the operating room performing surgical interventions for severe bullet and shrapnel wounds, amputating limbs as life-saving measures, and managing other traumatic injuries. We stopped only for short periods to rest and take light nourishment. It was a profound experience, testing not only my surgical skills and lifesaving decisions, but my endurance and ability to be in charge of a working staff during a crisis.

In this failed uprising to end Peron's dictatorship, more than 300 people were killed and over 1,000 wounded. None-the-less, the siege was the beginning of a new feeling of liberty in the hearts of the Argentinean people.

When the *Revolucion Libertadora* deposed the Peron regime a few months later, on September 16, 1955, I was already a junior member of the Surgical Department at the Fernandez Hospital in Buenos Aires.

Powerful and corrupt workers' unions had threatened retaliation against the medical staff because the regime's pictures, banners, sculptures and Peron-related emblems had been stripped from hospitals. I recall performing surgery at such times, when under my surgical gown, I could feel the weight of the 9 mm Luger semi-automatic pistol tucked into the waist band of my scrubs. This was hardly unusual since practically everybody was armed. Guns were easily available in the black market.

Thankfully, humorous events occasionally occurred which made the tension more bearable. Enrique was assisting in the operating room when the heavy weight of the Colt 45 semi-automatic weapon he'd thrust into his scrub pants pulled them down to his ankles. The pistol fell out part way through their descent and landed between his feet. For a split second everyone stopped breathing. Luckily, the safety was on and it didn't discharge. Relieved laughter erupted, and a nurse pulled up his pants and secured them to his undershirt with a surgical clamp. Enrique gingerly nudged the pistol under the operating table with the toe of his shoe. For months Enrique endured bawdy jokes about how his life might have been altered if the incident had turned out differently.

CHAPTER ELEVEN

The laughter of children running up and down stairs, bringing new signs of life to the old manor was gratifying. My parents truly enjoyed the many family get-togethers, trips to different places in New England, restaurant dining, and their three days seeing the highlights of New York City.

My father especially treasured the repeated outings to Boston's North End where we would walk along Hanover Street and the narrow back streets of the neighborhood. We stopped frequently so that he could chat in Italian with some of the older residents. On one of those trips, while enjoying an espresso at Café Vittoria, my father revealed a family event unknown to me or any of our other relatives.

In the late 1870's, my grandfather, Francisco DeNapoli arrived in Argentina accompanied by his young bride. They settled in the port city of Bahia Blanca, some 360 miles south of Buenos Aires. A tailor by trade, he soon established a thriving business. At the same time, his older brother left Chiusano di

San Domenico, their small village in the province of Avelino, Italy, for the United States, establishing his new residence in the Italian neighborhood of Boston's North End. Over the years, the brothers corresponded frequently, sharing their experiences of their adopted countries.

My father was born two years before the end of the nineteenth century, the seventh of ten siblings. Sometime in 1912, two of his oldest siblings and their father, traveled by ship to Boston to visit their uncle. My grandfather was very impressed by the city, the Italian neighborhood, and the friendly character of its people. All reminded him of his native Italy. With his brother's help, he researched the possibility of practicing his trade in the area. A positive response prompted him to make the decision to move to Boston with his family.

When he returned to Argentina, he immediately initiated procedures for admission to the United States, gathering his belongings and preparing for the projected trip. But the process of acquiring a permanent resident visa proved to be long and cumbersome. Over a year passed with delay after delay. In the meantime, rumors of war brewed, dividing the nations of Europe. When WWI broke out in June of 1914, traveling by ship became extremely ill-advised and dangerous because of German's submarines that prowled below the surface of the Atlantic

Reluctantly, my grandfather postponed his family's trip in the hope the war would soon end. However, by the time the conflict did end four years later, some of the older children had married, started their own families, and were firmly settled in Argentinean soil. By that time my grandfather was in his mid-fifties. He weighed all the variables, and felt too old for such a demanding venture, and unwilling to accept that not all of his family would accompany him. He regretfully discarded his dream. As the year's past, the family lost contact with our Boston relatives.

I was amazed when my father openly related these events, since my parents had always been reticent about reveling their family background, other than mentioning their place of origin and vague details about their ancestors' lives in Italy. It was their cultural style to be concerned about the present rather than to dwell on their ancestry. Perhaps a tinge of regret for what might have been made him wary of disclosing this episode of family's history.

I felt privileged to learn about my grandfather's long-ago trip to America. My father's message to his children was about living in the here and now. "Don't ground yourself in *if only - Act!*" was his message. But other experiences formed my father's understanding.

My grandfather lived with regret at being separated from his brother and not being able to reconnect. His choice was to lose part of the family he made or to lose the family he had been born into, along with his family's roots and remembered culture. His lesson to my father was, "endure as I have done."

My father made his own analysis and crafted his own message. "Acquire the skills you need to make your lives." I had heard an undercurrent to that message, "don't hold back." But I wondered if I'd heard the echo of the older generations.

All these familial disclosures gave me much to contemplate. I had seen myself as a pioneer of the DeNapoli family, the first to set foot on American soil. I owned this self-created identity for some time and used it as part of my motivational arsenal. My father's revelation shattered the simplicity of this idea but opened the path for another quest: to locate my relatives in or around Bean Town.

The two brothers of the last century tried to better the future of their young families by uprooting much of the familiar in their lives. Now I knew for certain there was a genetic component to my courage.

My older brother, Omar, a prolific short-story writer, used the new awareness of family history to delve into genealogy and was able to trace some of the family's past. He learned our mother had links with the House of Savoy, the royal reigning family in Italy from the eleventh century to the end of World War II. Her paternal uncle was *a Knight of the Kingdom*, second cousin to King Umberto I. With much difficulty Omar managed to obtain documentation that corroborated these facts. I began to wonder if my interest in Roman history for all these years might be grounded in some familial unconscious. But I was too much of the present and too busy to remain immersed in such musings for very long.

The warm satisfaction of my parents' vacation was shadowed, too soon after their return to Argentina, by looming dark clouds of anticipatory loss. A few months later, we received a letter from Omar with the sorrowful news that our father had been diagnosed with terminal cancer. It was imperative that Dolores and I travel to Buenos Aires. Since my father was hospitalized to receive treatment, we decided to stay in my mother's apartment to comfort and support her. After consulting with friends in the medical field, I had my father transferred to a private clinic specializing in cancer therapy. All medical interventions unfortunately proved futile in controlling the malignant process. My father passed away on May 18, 1967. Although I found consolation in remembering my father's visit, life seemed to be a roller coaster ride of the pairing of sorrowful and joyous events.

I was amazed at the web of life I was enmeshed within, seemingly revolving about me by reason of the responsibility for its well-being. I had always thrived on work but was mature enough now to realize the luck involved, over-and-above the myriad decisions I had to make on everyone's behalf.

Dolores was pregnant with our fourth child. I immersed myself in the joys of family life, finding comfort in the anticipation of another birth, but also in the older children's healthy growth and successful progress in school.

The commitment to my family meant involvement in Boy Scouts, field trips, PTO meetings, Little League games, and other extra-curricular activities. Later, on many occasions, the children would taunt me about my first Little League experience. J. Spencer, then 7 years old, had joined the neighborhood team and was to attend his first practice. I was on the field with the other fathers when the coach called for volunteers.

In Argentina, soccer is the national sport and baseball is non-existent, accounting for my total lack of knowledge of the game or its rules. However, I wanted to be an active participant, and approached the coach with the other fathers to offer my services. The coach, also a neighbor, gave instructions, directing me to be the first base umpire. Everyone moved to their assigned positions, but I remained rooted next to the coach. "You're the first base umpire," repeated the coach.

I sheepishly asked, "But where's first base?"

"Do you know anything about baseball?" the coach inquired with a friendly smile. "Not a thing," was the cheerful answer.

"OK, don't worry, Jorge. I'll teach you what to do."

The teaching continued over many practices and games, as I progressed in acquiring knowledge of America's favorite sport.

I had advanced in my profession and known throughout the area as a competent and well-respected psychiatrist. I had elevated the scientific standards at Baldpate, and my services were sought by nearby hospitals. With a successful professional reputation and a fairly large clientele, the time had come to climb another rung in the ladder to success.

I resigned my position at Baldpate and opened a full-time psychiatric practice in downtown Andover. I also joined the psychiatric staff at the newly opened Psychiatric Unit at Bon Secours Hospital in the neighboring town of Methuen, while at the same time, I became a member of the consulting staff at Lawrence General Hospital in the nearby city of Lawrence.

Shortly after, I was appointed Psychiatric Consultant at the prestigious Phillips Andover Academy, a position I was to hold for the next twenty years. My practice flourished medically and financially.

To secure financial protection for Dolores and the children, and to initiate my own retirement program, I consulted a lawyer friend, Richard F. O'Connor. We had met socially through the husband of one of Dolores' classmates. Richard had recently formed a financial consulting firm, The R.F. O'Connor & Associates Investment Company. I participated as one of the firm's original investors, and shortly after was named a member of the board of directors. Richard became my legal and financial adviser and we developed a close, friendly relationship.

In years to come, this relationship would play a significant role in being recruited by a covert government agency overseeing international security concerns.

Family, relatives and friends rejoiced as a second daughter, Melissa Dolores, our fourth child, was born on June 19, 1968 at Bon Secours Hospital in Methuen.

Because of the added demands maternal duties placed on Dolores's time, it was only appropriate that we made arrangements with relatives in Canada to sponsor a live-in, young nanny. Carol Robichaud, originally from a village outside of Quebec, came to occupy the third floor of 16 Hidden Road, which consisted of a bedroom, sitting room and bathroom. She was a charming, hard-working young lady with limited knowledge of English.

She almost immediately developed a loving relationship with the children, and gained the confidence and appreciation of everyone, practically becoming another member of the family. She had just celebrated her sixteenth birthday before leaving her Canadian home.

Building an in-ground swimming pool in the backyard enhanced the excitement of social activities. I arranged for my mother to visit, and she had arrived in time for the pool opening ceremony, becoming the first one to put her feet in the water.

Children in the neighborhood became regular users. The local YMCA used the pool three times a week for swimming lessons for its younger members. The manor at Hidden Road became the gathering place for most of our family, relatives, and friends' celebrations

The following year when classes ended in June, the entire family, except Melissa, too young to travel, flew to Buenos Aires so the children could know the land of their father's birth.

They were fascinated by the plane trip, especially the magnificent experience of flying over the Andes Mountain Range. During our visit, they learned about Argentina's historic sites, museums, and recreational destinations; and had the opportunity to get to know their South American uncles, aunts and cousins about whom they had only heard stories. Later, as teenagers, they would travel there alone on visits. Dolores and I also traveled to Buenos Aires every other year, to enjoy the company of friends and family.

Europe was a travel destination we had always hoped to experience. It would be to some extent a symbolic return to a home I had no personal memory of, but a place to which I was bonded by an idea of continuity.

Finally it became a reality when we received an invitation from Kristof and Monika to visit Munich. After an overnight flight from Boston, with a stop in Frankfurt, we landed on a breezy Sunday morning in mid-April. We were overjoyed to be together again, since it had been more than seven years since that tearful farewell on a New York City pier. On the drive to their home, the happy chatter was all about our lives, frequently interrupted by relating the accomplishments of our growing children.

Monika's second child, Gerhard, was already seven years old, while Melanie-Therese was a beautiful young lady of ten. We caught up through lunch and beyond, interrupted only by a telephone call inviting Kristof and Monika to dinner that evening to celebrate the Russian Orthodox Easter. Monika declined the invitation explaining that friends from the United States had arrived that morning. Upon the caller's insistence, however, she accepted the invitation to bring us along.

On that pleasant, warm evening, they drove us through picturesque Bavaria to our destination. We were surprised to pull up in front of a regal mansion on the outskirts of the city.

Dolores and I exchanged puzzled glances when the door was opened by a servant in full dress regalia, right down to his spotless white gloves.

A gathering of 10 guests conversed in the reception room, cheerfully anticipating a celebratory evening. The smiling host and hostess approached the entering guests and exchanged warm hugs and European style kisses with Kristof and Monika. They had obviously been friends for some time. They introduced themselves, welcoming us to their home, and expressing great appreciation for accepting the invitation to share the Russian Easter festivities.

I tried to hide my astonishment as I realized that we had entered a chapter of Royal European history. The heads of household were Natalya and Dmitri, of the House of Romanov, descendant of Nicholas II, the last Tsar of Russia, cousins of the tragically famous Princess Anastasia. (It might have been considerate of Monika to mention the type of evening we were to have, wouldn't it?)

Several white-gloved servers were offering a variety of hors d'oeuvres and flutes of champagne. When dinner was announced, the guests moved to a Renaissance-decorated banquet salon with a large, oval, dining-room table set for fourteen commensals.

Dmitri, the host, invited Dolores to take the seat next to Prince Sergei Andreevich, a Russian nobleman who spoke Russian and French. I was seated to the right of Princess Pilar, who spoke German and fluent Spanish. During our conversation, I learned that her full name was Maria del Pilar von Wittelsbach, Princess of Bavaria, descendant of Isabelle the Catholic, Queen of Spain; financier of Christopher Columbus's voyage to the new world.

Princess Pilar was a charming aristocratic lady who had never married. She lived with her personal servants in a wing of the Nymphenburg Castle in Munich, belonging to the Wittelsbach Royal Dynasty of Bavaria. The other parts of the castle were open to the visiting public.

Following an initial prayer led by Natalya, white wine was served with a side shot glass of Russian vodka. The *brindis*, in honor of the host and hostess, and to celebrate the Resurrection of Christ, consisted of a sip of wine followed by the shot of vodka.

The regal meal comprised numerous delicious courses and a variety of desserts, concluding with an Eastern Russian tradition where each guest selected an artfully decorated hard-boiled Easter egg, cracking it open against the egg held by the person to the left, and then eat it.

I had noticed that during the entire royally elegant celebration, all the other attendees addressed our friends as, *von Herrmann* and, *Grafin Monika*. My rudimentary knowledge of German made me aware that *Grafin* translated to countess. On the drive home, I boldly asked Monika if she were indeed of royal ancestry. With a big laugh, she admitted to being a descendant of the Wittelsbach Royal Family of Bavaria. She was not only a friend, but a distant relative of Princess Pilar.

"From now on should I address you as *Grafin,* or just plain *Mother Hen?*" I asked.

"I would really prefer *Mother Hen,*" replied Monika, and while everyone was laughing, she reached over and kissed me on the cheek. And over the years, *Mother Hen,* remained *Mother Hen.*

During the two weeks of our stay, we visited sites of the city, especially Marienplatz, the city's central square with its famous glockenspiel, a carillon on the Rathus Tower. At certain hours, red-coated figurines perform the cooper's dance (the barrel maker's dance) to commemorate the end of the plague in 1517. We also took trips to the Black Forest and the English

Gardens, stopping for a refreshing cold beer, or two, at one of the many *bierskellers* around the city.

Dolores was delighted to receive an invitation to join Princess Pilar, Monika, and other ladies, for an afternoon tea, at her residence, the Nymphenburg Castle. Dolores was enchanted long afterward with the experience, the details of which she recounted endlessly.

The highlight of the trip was a train ride to Salzburg, Austria, to visit the Nonnberg Benedictine Abbey, made known worldwide by *The Sound of Music* film in 1965.

For me, a guarded *highlight* was the re-enactment of a never-forgotten occurrence.

Sitting on the porch under the starry Bavarian sky, enjoying the cool breeze sweeping the Alps, Monika and I reminisced about the day's events while sipping glasses of Calvados.

Dolores and Kristof had retired for the evening. Our conversation grew increasingly seductive as we both contemplated the memories we'd buried from years before.

"Should we have lunch at Luchou's?" I blurted. Monika stood up and walked towards me. Without a word, her kiss lingered on my lips as she rested her head on my shoulder. We embraced tightly, her breasts and slender body pressing against mine.

"I love you, I'll arrange it," she whispered in my ear, hurrying back into the house. I remained on the porch, desire consuming my whole being. I slowly emptied the glass of Calvados. My heart pounded as I recalled the afternoon after Luchou's. For a brief moment, conflicting feelings troubled my mind. Was it love or just plain sexual desire? I dismissed the answer, and without guilt, accepted the yearning to be with Monika.

I had a restless night in anticipation of facing her at breakfast. My apprehensions were unfounded. Her warm smile and seductive look sent me a clear message. The long-ago promise was to be broken. *When and where?* was my mind's only thought; answered on the folded paper with the hotel address, she slipped into my hand

"Tomorrow afternoon at 2:00," she whispered.

The next day Dolores expressed her desire to visit an exhibit in a nearby Art Gallery. Kristof offered to accompany her to facilitate communication in the local language.

When the appointed time came for our *rendez-vous*, I took a taxi to a small hotel on Sonnenstrasse. She was already in the lobby when I arrived. Exchanging tender smiles, we climbed to the first floor holding hands. A number 6 on the door identified the nest for our passionate interlude.

For the remaining of our stay at their house, I was troubled with recurrent conflicting feelings of guilt and self-recrimination. We had broken our promise. But I had no doubt in my mind that my loyalty was to my wife and my family.

On our last day in Munich, Monika arranged for Dolores and me to travel by train to Passau, a picturesque town on the shores of the Danube, where we embarked on an excursion boat bound for Vienna. On Monika's recommendation, we stayed at the aristocratic Sacher Hotel, known around the world for its delicious Sachertorte, a famous chocolate cake, the pride of Viennese culinary specialties.

Arriving at the front desk, we were greeted by the concierge.

"Doctor and Mrs. DeNapoli, we have your reservations made by Grafin Monika." "*Mother Hen* has done it again," I thought with a smile.

Touring the enchanted city bathed by the not-so-blue waters of the Danube, we enjoyed its architectural splendor. We visited the Opera Haus, reminiscent of the musical tales of Mozart, Beethoven, Schubert, and Brahms; and Sigmund Freud's private office. We toured the Schonbrunn Castle; and marveled at the fine harmony of the classic dressage of the Lipizzaner horses at the Spanish Riding School.

On our last evening in Vienna, we took a taxi at the hotel entrance, directing the driver to the address of a restaurant suggested by the concierge.

"Ah, Americans," commented the driver. "No, no. Let me take you to one of the finest restaurants in Vienna!" he said and drove on to a hilltop on the outskirts of the city.

From the table by the window of the elegant restaurant, we had an overview of the city's lights, and the boats traveling on the Danube under the moon-lit sky. During the exquisite dinner, tuxedo-dressed violinists strolled by, playing magical Strauss waltzes, an appropriate finale for our fairy-tale adventure.

Back in the hotel suite decorated with all the grandeur of the renaissance period, we reminisced every moment of our first European experience. An unforgettable trip that had immersed us in the legendary splendor of royal life.

The next day, an airplane of the Lufthansa fleet brought us back to Boston, and to the routine reality of life in Andover.

CHAPTER TWELVE

Back home, an unexpected telephone call from Richard O'Connor would soon immerse me in the unknown world of back slapping, closed door machinations, and distorted representations; conduits to becoming a trusted public figure in the eyes of a certain electorate. I was about to enter the world of politics. Richard wanted to seek my advice about a personal matter. We met at the R.F. O'Connor & Associates' headquarters located in a Boston suburb.

Richard expressed his intention of becoming a candidate for a Massachusetts congressional district race in the November 1972 election. The seat would become vacant as the incumbent Republican was resigning after six consecutive terms in the U.S. House of Representatives to accept a governmental executive position in the Department of Commerce.

Richard would run as an independent against the well-established republican and democratic candidates.

"I'm not too well-versed in politics. How can I be of help to your campaign?" I wanted to know.

"You *are* an expert in human behavior, and your advice would benefit my team in designing behavioral strategies," replied Richard. I had always gravitated toward new intellectual challenges. I wasn't about to ignore the opportunity to test my capabilities in the adventurous field of promoting better political structures for my adopted nation. What I did not fully realize then was that my international experiences had uniquely prepared me for consideration in this national game of chess.

Richard had grown up in a conservatively democratic household, as were most of the Irish, Portuguese, and Greek residents of the district. But over the years his family had supported republican candidates as they disapproved of the increasingly liberal policies of the democrats. Even so, Richard was a newcomer in the arena; his dynamic personality was definitely an attractive quality to an electorate accustomed to an old fashion style of politics managed by a select circle, apparently not open to new ideas. He was charismatic and energetic, exuding enthusiasm, which he easily transferred to his management team and staff of volunteers.

Running as an Independent, he relied on contributions from campaign participants and a few outside sources. Apart from his personal resources, these were the only funds available.

Realistically, these monies were insufficient to run an effective campaign against the well- funded candidacies of his democratic and republican opponents who received full financial support and manpower from their respective central committees.

Richard's team conducted a door-to-door campaign distributing fliers and encouraging voters with prepared policy blurbs. In the many *O'Connor for U.S. Representative* rallies that were held, Richard shined as a fluent speaker with well-defined, middle-class policies.

It was a long and arduous contest that involved night-long strategy meetings and telephone discussions with Washington officials. As a member of the management team I was in charge of developing behavioral tactics such as posture, facial expressions, hand movements, response to questions, or reaction to heckling. All of this was aimed at enhancing Richard's image. I also had to establish liaisons with local and national strategists.

Two weeks before Election Day in November, the polls projected Richard to garner 13 percent of the votes. Not enough to win, but enough to impact the election's outcome. During one of the meetings of the management team at O'Connor's headquarters a phone call came in from a high official in the Republican Party in Washington. Richard, his campaign manager, and two of his strategists were invited by the GOP strategy committee to a discussion at the headquarters' office. The GOP provided travel expenses and lodging.

After a lengthy and heated evaluation of the implications of such a meeting, Richard decided to accept the offer, and appointed me as one of his strategists. This would be the first opportunity for me to share views with well-seasoned operatives in the Nixon Administration.

The trip to Washington was kept secret from the rest of the staff and the press. The debate and strategy meetings that took place were quite a comprehensive learning experience. I had never been exposed to the inner machinations of the political world, where principles were adulterated for the sake of compromise.

In accordance with the agreement reached with the Republican National Committee representatives four days before election day, Richard O'Connor announced his withdrawal from the race and declared his support for the republican contender. The GOP candidate won the seat in the U.S. House of Representatives by a 7 percent margin.

Far from satisfied with the capitulation, I had nevertheless learned invaluable lessons in closed-door dealings. More important, I had established personal contacts. I felt like I had passed Political Science 101 as an auditing student. I would learn later that others agreed in the evaluation of my performance. Everything I had learned would be of significance to my future in the political arena.

Except for the lingering resonance of my native tongue, I appeared to be a highly successful American doctor, increasingly busy in private practice, hospital work, and on the lecturing circuit. Energetic and positive enough in my attitude, I accepted a seat on the Board of Trustees of the Community Savings Bank in Lawrence. This position subsequently led to a place on the investment committee based on the experiences working with the R.F. O'Connor & Associates enterprise. Over the years, I had acquired considerable knowledge of banking and finance that had begun with the tutelage of Ken Whitton. I was also aware of how the economic stability of the country and controlled inflation contributed to the bountiful enhancement of my professional efforts. I realized I was a lucky man.

On the home front, Dolores continued her artistic endeavors with ardent zeal. She was an accomplished decoupage artist, a flower arrangement designer, and an active member of her book club. She was also a managing partner in the children's scholastic and sports activities, and she often volunteered in school-related events as a member of the PTA, or as a chaperone.

J. Spencer and Tiki were progressing well in their separate prep school studies in neighboring communities, and Deirdre, a well-adjusted and poised young lady, was completing her elementary education at Pike School in Andover. Melissa was coursing the fourth grade handily, despite her dislike for mathematics, immersing herself in her favorite artistic pursuit, the violin.

During our sons' prep school years, we participated in foreign student exchange programs that brought international excitement and gratification to the entire household. Cyrille, a teenage boy from Paris, France, was the first to spend time with us. The following year, his younger brother Fabrice, was our guest during the summer months, participating in community work in the area. Their sister Virginie also enjoyed our hospitality for several months, celebrating her fifteenth birthday while in our company. We communicated frequently with their parents, and years later, we finally met in person when Dolores and I visited their home in Paris, situated just off the beautiful Champs-Elysees.

I increasingly thought of myself as a citizen of the world. I had for some time actually attributed my dynamism to the celestial influence of having been born under the bright stars of the Southern Cross Constellation. This irrational belief was part of my family's lore from earlier days, and I had felt protected by forces beyond the realm of rational explanation for as long as I could remember. Apart from a normal reliance on intellectual thought, this was still my reality.

Our lives were very full, and many individuals would have sat back and enjoyed it, but I had one final step, to fulfill my own *cursus honorum*. This Latin term describes the succession of offices of increasing importance a man had to occupy and fulfill, in order to become a consul in the Roman Republic. Like feeling selected by the stars, leaning on the *course of honors* my ancient ancestors had put in place to ensure the best possible magistrates for Roman society, was a curious way for a man in the twentieth century to characterize his goals. But it did supply information as to what influenced my motivation, attitudes, and values. And so, in the midst of the full days, I methodically set aside 'study time' to prepare for the upcoming examinations to qualify as Board Certified in Psychiatry and Neurology.

Despite all our family and professional activities, Dolores and I enjoyed a busy social life. We fit in occasional trips to Washington D.C., Miami and New York City, my first American home. We took vacations with the children too, spending a month every summer renting a house on the beach in Seabrook, New Hampshire.

As parents, we reveled in having fun with the children. Dolores had been a champion roller skater during her high school years, but because of lower back and hip damage she suffered working as a nurse, she was fearful of aggravating old injuries by trying downhill skiing. I filled in during ski season, by driving the children every Sunday to the Waterville Valley ski area in New Hampshire.

I had lived my growing years on the shores of the Atlantic Ocean, far from the Andes Mountains. I had never learned to ski, witnessing my first snow fall during the internship in New York City. On our ski trips, the children would take lessons to develop their skills, while I enjoyed the warmth of the lodge, reading books about Roman History.

It was only a matter of time, watching from the lodge on a dazzling and invigorating wintry day when several inches of fresh powder graced the slopes, I was enticed to share in the fun. I had learned so many things. Couldn't a grown man learn to ski? On the next Sunday trip, I registered for lessons. At the designated teaching area, I found myself surrounded by a group of small children less than half my height.

"Are you the instructor?" questioned one of them.

"No," was my laconic reply, devoid of any further elaboration.

A young woman in her late teens joined us. She was the real skiing instructor. Approaching me with a buoyant smile she inquired, "Are you one of the fathers?"

Quietly, to hopefully avoid being heard by the children, I responded, "No, I'm here to take lessons."

"What's your name?" she asked.

"Jorge".

"Well Jorge, I'll be your personal instructor, and I'm sure you'll be the best student in my class."

I was far from convinced of the truth of her kind thought, but the initial lessons progressed to more advanced instruction. Eventually, I became a fairly competent skier. Some things are best learned young, but my skiing competency did enhance European vacations with the thrill of racing down trails in the Italian, Austrian, and Swiss Alps.

At the end of the summer of 1978, I passed the written part of the test for board certification. Three months later I successfully completed the oral portion, finally achieving board certified status. I exhaled completely for the first time I could remember.

The next interlude of my life was characterized by reaping the harvest of the years of preparation. My professional life was progressing smoothly; the family grew; J. Spencer and Tiki went off to pursue their college objectives. Word came from Ken Whitton that Dennis, too, had fulfilled his dream by being accepted as a plebe at West Point Military Academy.

The roller-coaster ride that is life continued its inexorable course re-routing my attention to important issues. Dismaying news from my youth's home put me in action mode. My elderly mother was to undergo major surgery for a suspected gastric tumor. I had to make immediate arrangements for a trip to Argentina. I had telephoned her physician who alerted me of the strong possibility of a malignant growth and the need for radical surgical removal.

In a family conclave, it was agreed that Dolores would remain at home with the children. J. Spencer, then almost 20 years old, would be her supportive partner while 18-year-old Tiki and I would travel to Buenos Aires for a few weeks.

It was a somber occasion. We stayed with my mother in the condominium I had purchased for her after my father's death. It was located on the fourth floor. My sister and her husband owned another unit, two stories above.

Tiki roomed with his same-age cousin, Sergio, in Omar's home. His house was only a short 15-minute bus ride away from my mother's place.

On the day of surgery, I was invited by the surgeon to witness the surgical intervention. I politely declined, as I had also declined to be present in the delivery room when the children were born. I could not emotionally tolerate seeing my mother undergo the expected extensive surgical procedure. I anxiously sat in the waiting area of the surgical unit, accompanied by Tiki, my sister Nora, and my brother-in-law Raul.

Having read my mother's medical chart, I knew from my own past surgical experiences that the outcome would be dim at best. This was clearly confirmed by the grave expression of the surgeon when he walked into the waiting area. Taking me aside, he explained in technical terms that the tumor was definitely malignant, extensive, and involved vital organs. Removal was impossible. He had done only a palliative procedure to alleviate pain; the predicted outcome was expected in only a matter of days.

Two weeks later, on our return flight to the U.S., I painfully recalled the moment I had personally discontinued life support measures, in agreement with the recommendation of the surgeon-in-charge, and with the consent of family members. As the only medical person in the family, I had accepted the burden of such responsibility. Years before, at my father's hospital bedside, on the medical advice of the treating physician, I had also agreed to stop the intravenous medication that was sustaining his life. It was a terrible privilege for me to be chosen as the family member to make these difficult decisions.

Tears of sorrow filled my eyes as I tried to cope with the irrefutable fact that life, without compassion, was inexorably severing my ties with my native country.

Within the next several years, our two sons graduated from college. The family also made the trip up the Hudson River to attend Dennis' graduation. This time, a proud smile marked the emotional impact as we watched The Long Gray Line march once more, now augmented by our own handsome friend stepping proudly along, one of the few black faces taking a place he had aspired to fill for so long.

It was a poignant day for me, reminiscing about how my understanding of racial awareness had grown and deepened. I had begun life in my adopted country, immersed in the underbelly of systems that hardly paid even lip service to offering the promise of American freedom and equality. I had lived through the times of social unrest in the sixties and I well knew the violence that often progresses in many forms, from ice picks to assassination. While witnessing a young man's dream of service to a country's ideal, a country that had denied opportunities to generations of his ancestors, I felt the peace of one man's resolve and forgiveness. Dennis' determination to offer himself in his country's service overwhelmed me with the power that a sense of personal honor conveys; to become the hope of possibility. It was profound and healing, reinforcing my father's lesson of the power of education in new ways.

Eventually, Dennis' father would retire as a full professor and return with his wife, Leah, to their hometown of Columbus, Georgia, on the shores of the Chattahoochee River. There, they would enjoy a changed environment where discrimination had lost much of its strength in the mainstream of life. There, amidst surroundings his ancestors had ensured with their sweat as much as any man's, Ken would run for a seat on the city council. The close friendship with this intelligent and thoughtfully committed man and his family had helped me to re-frame the bleak experience of those dismal conditions at Harlem Hospital, and the erroneous conclusions that had occurred to an angry young doctor.

What would come next? I expected to reach a position in life where events would progress smoothly to satisfactory resolutions. Both, J. Spencer and Tiki had left the homestead and had become self-supporting. Deirdre was attending the University of Granada, in Spain, for a study-abroad semester. Melissa was concluding her senior year of high school. J. Spencer was pursuing further studies in the field of *Informatica,* today known as computer sciences, and worked implementing a program of electronic management in a large Massachusetts hospital on the North Shore. Computer development was then in its infancy, and his skills in the field seemed to offer him a bright and successful future.

Tiki, more interested in the concrete, had entered the construction industry, specializing in home-building.

The next adventure for Dolores and me, with Melissa's schedule allowing her to join us, was visiting Deirdre in Granada and touring the fascinating cities of Spain.

At this stage, I had characterized our lives as *placid.* But that was not to last.

On his second campaign for office, Richard had been recruited by the National Republican Committee to be the candidate for a Massachusetts congregational district. Financial assistance, and the manpower to manage the campaign in an effective manner was provided. A swarm of pollsters, marketing experts, and political strategists practically invaded the O'Connor headquarters and once again, Richard had included me on his management team.

The Washington group conducted long informational sessions coaching the team in marketing techniques, speech content, and execution. The team re-learned the importance of physical appearance, behavioral manners, communication approaches, and nuances of speech delivery. We gained how-to information about organizing rallies and arousing group enthusiasm. We attended educational seminars in Washington and met with high-ranking advisers and legal experts, receiving instructions regarding fund raising and expenditures management. Information was provided about national security issues and Central Intelligence Agency operations affecting the campaign objectives. A number of sessions revolved around the other candidate's qualifications, background issues, pitfalls, and insider revelations.

I was repeatedly amazed at the level of sophistication and sagacious maneuvering in packaging and marketing Richard's candidacy. But time and personal effort expended, expert advice, instructional sessions, electors' rallies, and financial support proved to be of insufficient value. Richard O'Connor failed in his quest to unseat his democratic opponent.

At a post-election press conference, Richard announced his retirement from politics to concentrate his efforts on his corporate law practice.

As the routine of professional life moved along, I returned to investigate different behavioral approaches for the treatment of phobic conditions not responding to available conventional therapies. I had read about encouraging results obtained by using behavioral techniques promoted by a group of psychiatrists in Washington, D.C. who had recently organized themselves as a new entity, The Phobia Society of America. I traveled to meet them and joined the society as one of the first twenty charter members. I brought home to Massachusetts the new knowledge I acquired from attending several seminars; sufficient information to develop my own modified model to treat patients suffering from such disorders.

These frequent trips to Washington created appropriate opportunities to meet Mike from the Office of Strategic Information (OSI) on his own turf and discuss at length his offer to become an undercover operative.

Since his surprise phone call in the fall of 1980, the aura of intrigue associated with his proposal to participate in the Dogwood Chain had lingered in my mind. It wasn't in my nature to avoid a challenge, but I kept reminding myself to be cautious.

On one of these trips, I met Mike at Landon's Bookstore in the Georgetown Mall and we drove to area F in Bethesda, Maryland. There, I was introduced to two high-level operatives who questioned me intensely about my expectations and future plans. They already knew my life history. If I expressed a willingness to join them, and be accepted into the OSI, I would need to attend special seminars in counterintelligence to develop operational skills, learn elicitation techniques and ways to safeguard sensitive information; and how to identify high profile targets. If I accepted, traveling to Washington would have dual objectives: to refine the behavioral approach for the treatment of phobic conditions and to acquire information gathering expertise.

Over the next several months, I vacillated, weighing my options, considering and reconsidering the impact this decision might have on my life. How would the necessary duplicity affect relationships within my family? Would I be putting my professional life in jeopardy? Would I be able to keep these clandestine activities secret? What risks were involved? Why did I feel a certain compulsion to become involved? Could I trust the organization with my life? What about the security of my family? There would be no remuneration, only the satisfaction and pride of serving the nation. I could confide in no one. Some part of my subconscious worked over these questions incessantly.

One Tuesday, seated at my office desk after seeing the last patient of the day's schedule, the answer came clearly to my mind. With no hesitation, I lifted the phone and dialed Mike's number. The conversation was brief and to the point, "Yes, I will participate in the project." With a sigh of relief, I hung up; the anguish of deciding was over. I relaxed into the new reality. As I looked out the window at the clear blue sky, the date January 10, 49 BC came fully into my mind; a fateful day in the life of the Roman Republic. Like Caesar, I had crossed *my* Rubicon. "Alea iacta est". The die is cast. I only knew I had done it.

Three weeks later I was engaged in an intensive educational program of intelligence gathering. I was assigned a code name and instructed in code phrases and code questions to identify other links or external contacts. The only non-negotiable condition I had stipulated had been granted. I would receive no assignments in my native Argentina.

Mike would contact me regarding the first assignment. Months would pass before I heard from him again.

On the home front after the family's usual evening meal, the conversation was commandeered by Spencer's announcement of his marital intentions. Months before he had introduced to the family a co-worker, qualifying the relationship as a work-related friendship. Spencer was only twenty-one years old. He had always exhibited more maturity in his actions and reasoning than others of his age. He was conscientious, caring, and strong in his attachment to the family. His initial surprising disclosure was followed by a second, shocking statement. His future bride was in her third month of pregnancy.

Parents have certain expectations based on their values and their assumptions about the course lives normally take. We had dreams of exuberant gatherings of relatives and friends to celebrate the beginning of the happy occasion of seeing each child marry. We shamelessly viewed such events as the joyful precursor to the arrival of grandchildren. This rite of passage insured and validated the continuation of the giving and receiving of love their parents had shared. Spencer's unexpected revelation brought misgivings. These misgivings were reinforced in further discussions by Spencer's assertion that, "I like my wife-to-be, but I'm not in love with her."

Misgivings now became concerns. Neither Dolores nor I could reason with him, dissuade him, or convince him that errors flawed his thought processes. Further discussions were of no avail. I could foresee that Spencer's and his bride's dissimilarities would be disruptive to their adjustment to married life. She was 11 years older, and her social sophistication and intelligence did not match Spencer's. Their relationship was conflicted and dispassionate from its very beginning.

As the years passed, a girl and two boys were born from this misfit union. Spencer confessed to us that he felt manipulated and deceived in their conception. He loved his children and had strong feelings of responsibility in providing for their emotional and physical welfare. He postponed the dissolution of the marriage for years but eventually filed for divorce, though he continued to provide for their financial support and to care for them on alternate weekends and yearly vacations. He invested himself as well in both time and interest in their educational development.

Months after his divorce, Spencer moved into his own apartment in Boston, concentrating on his own career in the electronics industry.

Meanwhile, Tiki prospered in his building enterprise with a side interest in the music business. His passion for skiing attracted him to the mountains of Vermont, and he eventually settled in the Mad River Valley.

Melissa followed her brother's footsteps, establishing her home in Warren, Vermont. Her ambition was to enter the hotel hospitality industry. At first, she supported herself working as a server in a local restaurant until she was able to secure a position as a customer-relations concierge at the prestigious Pitcher Inn, member of the Relais & Chateaux chain. The Inn was located in the picturesque village of Warren at the foot of Lincoln Peak. Melissa was a persuasive and constructive communicator and negotiator who loved her work.

Deirdre had graduated from Simmons College with a double major in psychology and Spanish, based on language skills she acquired while studying abroad at the University of Granada. She continued in post-graduate studies towards a master's degree in Psychology while working as a counselor at Bournewood Psychiatric Hospital. She shared a condo in Boston with a college classmate.

With the children no longer living at the manor, we had expanded our social life and activities, taking more frequent vacations to visit friends and relatives in cities in South America and Europe, and exploring new horizons in the Caribbean. The purchase of time-shares in Aruba allowed us to spend the coldest weeks of winter bathing in warm waters.

Most of the traveling to cities around the world was related to expanding my educational goals, attending medical and psychiatric conferences, or lecturing at international locations. The destinations of these study trips were not really chosen at random, though they might have appeared to be. Mike kept in close contact with me, organizing the educational journeys to countries and cities where I could conduct my assigned duties of information gathering.

Overcoming my initial apprehensions, I built enough confidence to become a productive operative in undercover work; receiving praise from unidentified superiors, through

Mike, my only liaison to OSI headquarters. They were particularly satisfied with the degree of detail I provided, and human insights offered.

As the last two years of the 1980s were to be placed on the shelf of the past, significant changes would occur in the DeNapolis' life.

The warmer breezes of the early spring of 1989 caressed the belongings of the manor being loaded into the trucks of a moving company, ready to transport them to our new home on the shores of the Merrimack River.

The children were all leading independent lives. This reality had hastened the expected inevitability of mid-life adjustments. Alone in the manor, Dolores and I concluded the time had come to move to more manageable quarters. After months of searching neighboring communities we finally had settled on a two-bedroom townhouse with a magnificent river view. The new home was one of 18 units in a newly built condominium complex in the town of Amesbury, near the New Hampshire border. The new home was ideally located between two major highways, within easy driving distance from Boston and just twenty minutes away from my office in Andover.

Our tranquil existence, with its overlook on the often-soothing river's waters, was a dramatic change from the previously buzzing life at the old manor. Gone were the pool parties, the social gatherings to celebrate family and friends' special occasions, the yearly patriotic and Christmas festivities. Life took a more relaxing tone but was still busy with social events and other commitments. Also, the longing to travel to foreign countries fit more easily into the new, less demanding schedule. Needless to say, it would also perfectly accommodate my undercover activities.

One important operation took place during one of our frequent vacations to Aruba, in March of 1992. In anticipation of the assignment, my anxiety was at a high level but within tolerable limits. I was determined to successfully complete my mission.

On previous trips I had befriended Dr. Jaime Falconi, a neurologist on the staff at Horatio Oduber Hospital, the health facility on the island. His wife Nivia belonged to a prominent Aruban family. She was related by marriage to Olindo Koolman who had been appointed governor by Queen Beatrix of The Netherlands.

Hugo Chavez' rising socialistic movement in Venezuela, and his relationship with Fidel Castro in Cuba, was impacting the future operation of the Coastal Aruba refinery in the city of San Nicolas in the eastern end of the island. El Paso Corporation of Texas had taken over Coastal Oil Company in 1991. Petroleum from Venezuela was a valuable commodity for the United States and the Netherlands.

My relationship with Jaime and Nivia Falconi progressed into a life-long friendship, as the information obtained from official sources during social visits to the governor's mansion benefited the Dutch government in its negotiations with the neighboring countries of Cuba and Venezuela. Sometimes I had a sense of the general worth of my contributions relative to long-term assignments. At others I completed assignments without any grasp whatsoever of what use my efforts might contribute.

Our visits to Aruba resulted in Dolores and I becoming close friends with a group of vacationers from Akron, Ohio, especially Luke and his wife Sonia. Luke was a chemical engineer, owner of an industrial chemical plant on the outskirts of the city. His hobby was constructing miniature remote-controlled mechanical devices.

Our friendship extended beyond the time spent together in Aruba. We visited in our home cities and traveled together to European destinations on a number of occasions. Luke had an inquisitive mind yearning to understand the complexities of the world by engaging in adventurous endeavors.

As I became more familiar with Luke's behavioral mode, I began to suspect that there was an ulterior motivation attached to his interest in mechanical devices and his traveling pattern. I had witnessed the same trait pattern in other trainees at the OSI. We trained in groups of two or three, but never knew their names as we only used code names.

One lazy day, as the last rays of the colorful Caribbean sunset cast elongated shadows of the palm trees over the sand, Luke and I savored our customary late-afternoon martinis while relaxing on comfortable lounges. This had become a daily ritual while on vacation and I was rather particular about its preparation. Tanqueray martini on the rocks, dry, with three olives, in a snifter. I would even hand servers and bartenders printed cards, to their amusement and delight, describing my preference. Perhaps a little James Bond coursed through my veins, after all.

That late afternoon, I thought was the appropriate time to unravel the mystery if one existed. I addressed Luke with a code sentence followed by a code question. Luke's eyes widened in shocked recognition. He faked a coughing spell and took another sip of his Martini, then he extended his hand and uttered a code greeting.

"You must be shitting me!" he blurted with a big laugh. "How long have you been on the chain?" We continued to jovially exchange all sorts of work-related questions, interrupting each other and laughing like two mischievous kids re-living their escapades. At last I had someone with whom to share my undercover experiences.

Our friendship was never the same since it took on another dimension as our relationship deepened. We agreed to contact our respective liaison agents to investigate the possibility of sharing assignments. The request would be granted and years later we would find ourselves together in the riskiest performance of our clandestine careers.

CHAPTER THIRTEEN

The upcoming wedding approached as a blissful event for Dolores and me. Deirdre and Peter F. Dunn had been sweethearts since their student days together at Brooks School, a private preparatory school in North Andover, Massachusetts. They had been committed to each other in many ways for many years.

Peter had completed his undergraduate degree and was now finishing his senior year at George Washington University Medical School in Washington, D.C. He had grown up in an Irish household with strong family ties and deep religious beliefs. His parents were long-time residents of Andover. Two married sisters lived in adjoining communities.

Deirdre and Peter had planned their wedding for months, with Dolores and Deirdre in charge of making everything happen. They had even arranged with the new owners at 16 Hidden Road for the newlyweds to have their wedding pictures taken on the curved staircase in the home where Deirdre had grown up.

Deirdre beamed with happiness as she glided down the church aisle in her elegant white gown. I beamed as well as I escorted her into her new conjugal state.

One of the highlights of the wedding was Dolores's 89-year-old father's participation; he was elegantly dressed in a long-tailed tuxedo, and walked the mother of the bride, flanked by her two sons, to the family pew at the front of the church. Most missed was Dolores's mother, who had passed away ten years before; however, she was surely with us in spirit.

I thought of my own parents, finally understanding all they had wished to instill and synthesize into the future through that bookshelf in our old dining room. How far those few volumes had carried me!

The newlyweds made their first home in Washington, D.C., giving us the opportunity to travel to the city and visit them frequently. While living in Washington, Deirdre became pregnant with their first child, prompting them to move to a larger apartment across the Potomac River in Alexandria, Virginia. Matthew was born there, and a second son, Chandler, enlarged the family two years later.

Even the happiest of times often coincides with tragic events as the generations overlap. Blest are those families whose generations come and go in natural progression, so the younger generation says good-bye to the older and the older shares the joy of glimpsing their family's future. Shortly after Deirdre's first pregnancy, Dolores's father died suddenly of a heart attack at the age of 91, coincidentally, or by God's design, on his late wife's birthday. The loss of this gentle, loving man, mentally alert and self-sufficient to his last day, was profound for the whole family. He always showed love and interest in the happenings of all his children, especially his grandchildren and great-grandchildren.

After graduation from medical school Peter completed a one-year surgical internship and two years of surgical residency at George Washington University Medical Center, significantly expanding his surgical abilities. He then finished a two-year research fellowship in the National Institutes of Health in Bethesda, Maryland before the Dunn family fulfilled their desire to return to Massachusetts. By then, Peter wanted to pursue a career in critical care requiring him to first complete a three year residency program in anesthesia. He won acceptance to the program at Massachusetts General Hospital in Boston, successfully accomplishing his goals.

Peter, a highly intelligent young man, was dedicated to his profession and determined to achieve significant goals in his career. His efforts were rewarded with a rapid climb to an academic vice-chairmanship position in the anesthesia department, usually reserved for a more seasoned professional. Peter's academic and financial success allowed the couple to purchase their first home, where they welcomed two more children, Morgan and Madison, born two years apart.

Their house, located in a new development in a residential area of North Andover, became the new center for social events, family gatherings, and festive holiday celebrations. The torch had been passed; Deirdre had become the official family hostess with Dolores comfortably assuming a more matriarchal role.

I too, had begun to abrogate some of my responsibilities by welcoming into my busy private practice a part-time board certified psychiatrist, a full-time psychologist, and two psychotherapists with masters degrees in Social Work. Additional professional help allowed me a more flexible schedule and more time away from the office. Administrative and financial aspects of the practice were skillfully managed by Patricia, my trusted office manager, who had been my *Girl Friday* since shortly after the establishment of my practice 25 years earlier.

All through the 1990's, Dolores and I traveled extensively. Yearly trips to Buenos Aires kept us connected with family and friends. January vacations in Aruba with the children and grandchildren allowed us to enjoy the next generation in pleasant surroundings. Multiple European trips to new and old destinations fulfilled our personal agendas.

My enrollment in educational seminars and medical psychiatric conferences, as well as lecturing engagements, were always linked to undercover commitments. I participated in information-gathering ventures in cities such as Vienna, Prague, and Paris. The clandestine work took place during driving tours of Provence in Southern France, art shows in Marseille, and while partaking of the fine cuisine of Lyon, the gourmet capital of the world. In that particular tour, Dolores's brother Norman and wife Carol accompanied us, giving me the flexibility to absent myself at opportune times.

An assignment from Mike took us to the Czech Republic and Slovakia where we enjoyed a fabulous vacation. We had invited our good friends John and Carolyn Simko to join us. This trip was of special interest to John whose late father was originally from Slovakia

While making arrangements for our Munich-Bratislava-Prague trip, I had contacted the Munich Chamber of Commerce inquiring about the route of the famous Bavarian Oktoberfest Parade through the streets of Munich and the hotels located along the route. The clerk at the office recommended the Hotel Daniel on Sonnenstrasse, a family owned and moderately priced three-star hotel. I had called in advance and made the necessary reservations.

Dolores had telephoned Monika advising her of our impending visit, declining her offer to meet us at the airport as we were to land very early in the morning. Arriving at the Munich International Airport we hired a taxi to transport us to the Hotel Daniel. As we entered the lobby my heart started pounding wildly as I recognized the place where my sexual encounter with Monika had occurred years before.

At the front desk, John and Carolyn were given the key to number 9, an inside room.

Dolores and I were registered in room 6 on the first floor, overlooking the street; the very room of my previous liaison. I suddenly was face-to-face with the convergence of two aspects of my life I had always been able to hold apart both within my mind and heart.

I felt no guilt over this duality. I saw no duplicity in my behaviors; my personal identity tended toward Italian conventions, as I understood them, all the way back to the heroic Romans; yet I could not possibly share that room with Dolores. To do so would blur boundaries I *did* feel, whether or not I chose to acknowledge or understand them. I felt a male right to exercise passion at will. At the same time, I was certain Dolores and I did not belong together in that room. My wife's place was different. Not sacrosanct, but separate.

"Since this is John and Carolyn's first visit to Munich, they should occupy the street-front room." I said nonchalantly, as I took the key from John's hand for room 9 and exchanged it with mine.

Why is destiny mischievous with our feelings? I wondered.

Hours later while visiting with Kristof and Monika, she inquired where were we staying. When Dolores mentioned the Hotel Daniel, Monika's facial expression remained unchanged, but seconds later she gave me a look of disapproval, questioning,

"How did you select your hotel?" I related the recommendation from the Chamber of Commerce and commented with a suppressed smile, "I should have consulted you." Apparently Monika also thought Dolores did not belong in that room. I noted her annoyance, but I did not trouble myself with its implications.

And yes, it did happen! Monika and I chose once again to be together; to share our passion once more in what I thought of as the primary affirmation of being alive.

"Love is a thing that is never out of season," said English poet Barry Cornwall (Bryan Waller Procter's pen name), which leaves to the individual whether this *thing* might possess licit and illicit aspects, even among self-actualized adults.

The four of us spent a week in Munich with our old friends Kristof and Monika during the Oktoberfest, and two days in Bratislava, a four-hour train ride away from Munich. There we visited the small village of Andrejova near the border with Poland, where John's father was born. Two more hours on the train and we arrived in Prague, which I consider to be one of the five most beautiful cities in the world. I would visit Prague on three more occasions, one of those with my friend Luke.

In Prague, I met my contact, code name Jellika, a Polish national. She was a beautiful woman in her 40's with years of experience in the antics of espionage. In subsequent assignments we would develop a more than close relationship, expressed at the times we were thrown together, since we had mutually agreed not to communicate outside our assignments. I never even knew her real name.

At one time I had asked Mike, if while traveling to England on a future trip, I would be able to visit the British Secret Intelligence Service (SIS) known as MI6, headquartered at the

Century House on Westminster Bridge Road in the borough of Lambeth. Mike consulted with his superiors and returned with an affirmative answer.

The opportunity finally came. As a consultant for the Psychiatric Institute of America (PIA), a private enterprise with offices in Washington, I had been commissioned in October of 1994 to meet in Paris with the French Vice-Minister of Health to learn about their national health system as it applies to mental health issues.

Dolores was delighted to go to Paris again, and more so, when I suggested we extend the trip by beginning with a four-day stay in London. During our stay there we visited Buckingham Palace, St. Paul's Cathedral, the Tower of London, and opulent Chelsea. Also, Spencer Square, and the bohemian Notting Hill. We enjoyed the sights of black taxis, red mailboxes on street corners, and red telephone booths. Riding the upper level of the two-decker buses was very exciting. As a memento, we had our picture taken at the monolith marking the zero-degree longitude of the Greenwich Meridian.

Dolores was surprised that I would be interested in going to the SIS offices alone, but settled for a shopping excursion to Harrods Department Store and other chic boutiques. I spent most of the day visiting Century House.

My interest was aimed at the new and different approaches to behavioral profiling and elicitation that the British were implementing. It would also intrigue my friends, especially Luke, that I had been in the innermost hub of the British Secret Service.

On the following morning, I took the *tube* to the Lambeth North Underground Station and walked to the SIS operations training center next door.

Washington had informed them of my expected arrival. Security was tight. At the entrance checkpoint, I had to pass through a metal detector, and leave my passport and cell phone. I was given a picture ID visitor's pass and was accompanied by an armed guard at all times. I was quite impressed by the friendliness, professionalism, and skills of the men and women in the British Service. What I learned improved my skills in the difficult and sensitive field of profiling and counterintelligence. Retrieving my passport and cellular, I left the headquarters with a valuable amount of knowledge and an understanding of their operative style.

At the last minute we changed our plans, and instead of flying to Paris, decided to take the Train a Grande Vitesse, traveling under the English Channel. While riding through the English countryside and in the tunnel, the train reached speeds of 85 miles per hour, but on the French railroad system it sped up to 186. It was an amazing experience. In 2 hours and 15 minutes we entered the station in Paris, arriving within 10 seconds of the scheduled time.

I had three days of continuous conferences with Monsieur Pierre Tandreaux, the Vice Minister of Health, recording the interviews for a presentation at the Psychiatric Institute forum upon my return.

We spent the rest of our stay walking the streets of Montmartre and the intellectual Montparnasse, the avenue of the Champs-Elysees with its cinemas, outside cafes, and aristocratic residences. We savored tea and pastries at Stephanie's Tea Room on rue Rivoli, across from the Louvre, and white wine with foie gras at the Café de la Paix, overlooking the Opera House. On previous trips to the City of Light, we had visited landmarks like the Eiffel Tower, Arc de Triumphe, Notre-Dame Cathedral, the Louvre Museum, and other tourist sites. Most attractive to me was the fact that Paris, oblivious to other cultures, was 100 percent French.

As was our custom in every visit to Paris, we reunited with the Couadous, parents of the exchange students that had spent time at 16 Hidden Road. When Cyrille, Fabrice, and Virginie found out that we were visiting their parents, our briefly adopted children quickly converged at their parents' home to greet us. It was a most happy and enjoyable occasion.

As the Air France plane departed, we could hardly contain our feelings of nostalgia, as we had always felt at home in the streets of Paris.

CHAPTER FOURTEEN

Life was about to change. Unexpected and disturbing news came in the form of a phone call from Spencer who said that he needed to see us. Our children usually just dropped by, they didn't call for appointments. I was sure he had sounded upset. What could be wrong? We were worried before he arrived, anxious to listen to his concerns. He initially began by making, what seemed to be, superfluous comments about his health. I was puzzled. Spencer was only thirty-five. At 6'3", and 225 lbs. he appeared to be a model of fitness.

Spencer, visibly uncomfortable, tried to articulate whatever it was he had come to say, perhaps empathizing with how hard his words would be for us to hear. He stumbled verbally, and then got it out. He said that a month before, while showering, he had discovered a lump in his left armpit. His doctor referred him to a surgeon immediately. A pathologist friend of mine did a biopsy of the node removed from his left axilla and made a conclusive diagnosis of non-Hodgkin lymphoma, a malignancy of the lymph system closely related to leukemia.

Even though Spencer had not experienced any symptoms, there was already a possibility that the disease had spread to his bone marrow and other organs. He had been referred to the Oncology Department of Boston City Hospital for further evaluation and to establish a treatment plan.

J. Spencer DeNapoli.

Spencer had already told his brother and sisters. The devastating report washed over the family like an icy wave. The whole family rallied to support him. Facing things together was a DeNapoli family style forged around the dinner table, night after night, discussing serious news or casual events. We were a team. Everyone wanted to do something to contribute to Spencer's recovery, but at the moment there was little to do since he was symptom-free. In fact, he was having a hard time realizing he was as sick as his doctors reported, so he continued to work and manage his life as before.

Dolores and I went with him to his initial evaluation at Boston City Hospital. I had researched several oncology departments through my professional resources, and was satisfied that Spencer would be getting the most highly-rated care available in New England.

While hospitalized for three days for a complete work-up, his team of doctors determined that Spencer's treatment would be done on an out-patient basis and would consist of oral anti-cancer medications, preventive antibiotic therapy and weekly intra-venous chemotherapy. The weekly infusion treatments would last approximately four hours. We would drive him to Boston City Hospital for his treatments.

Since Spencer was still able to work full-time, the sessions were scheduled for Friday mornings, giving him time to recover over the weekend from any side-effects. After three months of chemotherapy, he showed an excellent response with no evidence of cancer cells in repeated blood tests. He would continue his oral anti-cancer regimen, and because his immune system was compromised, daily antibiotics were prescribed.

A year later he was still cancer-free, feeling physically well and quite optimistic in his outlook. Treatment was temporarily discontinued, with monthly follow-up visits. Over the next year Spencer felt enthusiastic about his recovery, making long-term plans for his career and for his children's education.

But cancer is a formidable invader and other skirmishes lurked in the most remote part of Spencer's life force. Once again he began to feel increasingly fatigued, then feverish. A chest x-ray revealed an infectious pneumonic process requiring immediate hospitalization. Subsequent blood tests showed a re-appearance of lymphoma cells, necessitating the re-introduction of chemotherapy.

This time his recovery was not as spectacular or as complete as after the first round. His progress was slow, marred by episodic relapses and gradual, general deterioration. Frequent bouts of pneumonia required repeated hospitalizations.

He managed to care for himself in his Boston apartment, but could no longer cope with the stress and responsibilities of his job. With great regret, he applied for medical disability leave.

As time progressed, his condition fluctuated from short periods of well-being to frequent relapses. His immune responses continued to erode. Everyone was aware that Spencer was incrementally losing his fight against the malignant enemy. Yet, he continued to present an optimistic front, reassuring family and friends that he wasn't ready to give up the fight. He expected each future remission would be long-lasting while hoping for new, break-through treatments.

It was Spencer's nature to always be more concerned about those around him than to fixate on his own situation. He never complained about his symptoms or physical limitations, and even when complications required hospitalizations, he always remained positive. Even at his worst moments he kept his sense of humor.

Throughout his illness, he never neglected his parental responsibilities, visiting his children often and showing interest in their scholastic achievements. In private conversations, he told me how much he regretted his inability to be a full-fledged father due to the limitations his disease placed on his personal reserves of energy.

Spencer courageously fought the dreadful illness for five years. People celebrate little successes all the time, but the arsenal of conversational words to mark steady decline is meager. When he began to require the aid of a cane to walk, just the slightest downturn of shoulders acknowledged his loss. Soon he reached a point where he was unable to drive.

During twice weekly visits to Spencer's apartment in Boston, we would walk to a small corner restaurant for dinner. We enjoyed these get-togethers, indulging in nostalgia, laughing over happy times now past, and mischievous episodes previously unshared with parents.

His children continued to visit him often, many times driven by me.

It was important to Spencer to remain independent as long as possible. On Christmas day 1998, I drove to Boston and brought him to his sister Deirdre's home for the holiday dinner. After-dinner conversation turned to our annual vacation time in Aruba. Spencer was adamant that we should proceed with our plans for the vacation, scheduled for departure on January 2nd.

Reluctantly, we left even though we had profound concern over Spencer's progressively failing health. I had contacted his attending physician who reassured me that even though Spencer's condition was declining, no major relapses were expected in the next several months.

From away in Aruba, we could assess the situation more realistically. Overwhelmed by feelings of sadness and anticipated loss, we realized the inexorable truth that Spencer was losing his fight. In a cruel way, life was clipping his wings in mid-flight, only months before his 40th birthday. We understood that all his dreams and ambitious plans would fade into non-existence.

A week into our tormented *vacation*, a phone call from Peter confirmed our fears. Spencer had suffered a major setback, complicated with double pneumonia, requiring emergency admission to the intensive care unit.

I contacted the airline, but all flights were booked for the next week. The huge sense of dread was somewhat mitigated by a call to my friend, Doctor Falconi. A friend of his, a member of the executive board of American Airline's Aruba office, made seats available on a flight leaving the next day.

Deirdre and Peter were waiting when we arrived at Logan Airport. We drove directly to the hospital. Spencer greeted us weakly with a big smile. His breathing was labored, his voice barely audible. "You should have stayed in Aruba. I'll get over this setback." I was overwhelmed. *He has the same optimistic attitude, even now,* I marveled.

Over the next two weeks, we spent most of our time with him. Tiki and Melissa had come from Vermont to be near, too, and were staying with friends in Andover.

As Spencer's life ebbed away, progressive respiratory failure made it necessary to intubate him as he drifted in and out of consciousness. During briefly lucid periods, he communicated by writing notes on a clipboard. Once he wrote, "I'm not giving up." His body was failing but his spirit was very much alive.

Eventually, he lapsed into a deep coma. The end loomed. A respirator and IV medication keeping his heart functioning were all that sustained life.

His doctor called for a family meeting to discuss the next course of action. He explained that because of continuous intubation and artificial breathing, Spencer had developed Irreversible Respiratory Distress Syndrome, a common complication in his condition. The options were clear: to keep him on the respirator for an indefinite period of time knowing that there was no chance of recovery or discontinue life support measures.

On the afternoon of January 25th, 1999, Dolores, Deirdre, Peter, Tiki, Melissa and I, met in the ICU waiting room. We were all somber. Some of us wept at facing the most difficult of decisions. Peter took the initiative, accustomed as he was in dealing with similar situations in his professional work, when medicine finally fails. As I expected, Peter suggested discontinuing life support. I was grateful I did not have to recommend it myself. I strongly supported Peter's suggestion, knowing it was the course of action that had to be taken. One by one, all the others agreed to let Spencer die in peace.

I told the nurse-in-charge of our decision, and she informed Spencer's doctor who arrived within minutes to talk with the family and write the official order. Before leaving he expressed his regrets that the efforts to restore Spencer's life had been unsuccessful.

The family congregated around Spencer's bed. Dolores was the first to kiss his forehead and say her goodbyes. The others followed in turn. They all had left the room, and I was alone when the nurse entered to discontinue the IV medication keeping his heart alive. I asked her to let me stop the IV infusion. I mentally addressed my grown child, *My son, I gave you life and now I am taking it away to let you die in peace. God be with you.* Tearfully, I shut off the IV. I called Dolores and the children back into the room, and we somberly watched the monitor record the gradual slowing of his heart tracing until the line became flat. It took almost an hour until Spencer entered eternity at 10:02 pm.

In the hospital parking lot, the family clustered in the chilly air of the cold night. Dolores released the *Get Well* balloon that had been tied to the foot of Spencer's bed. We watched as it rose higher and higher between the tall buildings, finally disappearing out of sight.

Spencer was buried in the family plot in West Parish Garden Cemetery, in Andover, less than a mile from my office. We could never have imagined that our first-born child would be the first to be interred there.

For the next six years, until my retirement from practice, I visited Spencer's grave almost every lunchtime. There, at least, the emptiness of that part of my life dedicated to my son could be borne.

I still frequent the area regularly, dropping by to talk to him. I miss the opportunity to feel this connection when I am away.

Years later, during a television interview to discuss the newest treatment approach for complex anxiety disorders, I was asked, "What was the most difficult thing you've had to do in your life?" Without hesitation I responded, "To bury my son."

For unknown reasons following their divorce, Spencer's ex-wife kept a distant relationship with our family, not allowing the children to participate in family gatherings in spite of repeated invitations from Dolores and Deirdre. She seemed to feel they were now only *her* children. Foolish woman. As the grandchildren grew older, Dolores often contacted them in an attempt to bring them closer to the family. We had taken them out to dinner on their birthdays and at Christmas time, but their emotional attachment became tenuous over the years.

My grief was compounded by receiving news that my good friend Enrique had passed away only ten days before Spencer. His wife had been reluctant to burden me with the bad news at the same time that I was dealing with Spencer's final moments.

In our frequent communications, Enrique Casanello, aware of Spencer's terminal disease, had never mentioned his own struggle with lung cancer, wanting to spare his friend the pain of another imminent loss.

CHAPTER FIFTEEN

Another year passed, and with the arrival of the millennium, the painful sadness of illness and powerlessness gradually diminished, replaced by warm memories of Spencer's life.

With the showers of the Vermont spring a new romance had flowered, too. Tiki announced his intention to marry his longtime girlfriend. The wedding would take place the following summer on the grounds of his friend Bryant Fitzgibbons's Estate, *The Farm on the Mad River,* in Waitsfield, Vermont. By that time, Tiki would have celebrated his 41st birthday. He thought the time had come to settle down and start a family.

Family and friends gathered on *The Farm on the Mad River* for the civil ceremony. It was a joyous family occasion with live music provided by musician friends of Tiki. The festivities, including music, dancing and libation, lasted two days as many attendees from out of town stayed at local inns scattered along the length of the beautiful, green *Mad River Valley.*

As a natural consequence of being in the construction industry, Tiki had built his own house on a nine-acre parcel of land halfway up the mountain with a breathtaking view of distant peaks and lush forests.

Tiki and his bride had started strong, and believed they were ready to settle down and raise a family. A son, Domenic Spencer, was born two years later; and Nina Bel increased their joy at her arrival just before Domenic's fourth birthday.

Tiki is a jovial and hardworking man who enjoys his children and being a father. But emotional conflicts, poor communication, and mutually unrealistic expectations progressively led to an untenable situation. The couple agreed that terminating the marriage was best. Tiki was able to keep the house for the enjoyment of the children on their weekend visits. Eventually, he found another emotionally rewarding relationship that brought happiness and fulfillment to his life.

He visited our home quite frequently, affording us the chance to enjoy a loving and harmonic closeness with our grandchildren.

Travel abroad was a continuous topic of interest and conversation. Becoming a citizen of the world through travel experiences had become the natural consequence of all the years of reading world history. The possibilities of travel would never become banal. In one of their frequent telephone communications, Dolores had suggested to Sonia that she and Luke should join us on a 16-day river cruise through the waterways of Europe, sailing from Vienna to Amsterdam. Sonia agreed to discuss it with Luke and give the final answer. Luke readily agreed and within weeks we had embarked on a storybook vacation, with limited government business this time.

Landing in Vienna, we ate dinner that night at the well-known Frauenhuber Café on Himmelportgasse, before boarding the river ship *Rhapsody*. We traversed the Danube, Main, and Rhine Rivers, docking in small quaint towns and large cities. In one of them, Nuremberg, we felt the palpable reminder of the justice which had been meted out in the post-World War II Nazi trials. In Frankfurt and Cologne, where remnants of Roman heritage were manifest throughout the city, Luke and I enjoyed the fantasy of transporting ourselves through past times, the clank of Roman armor resonating through our imaginations. A side bus trip took us to the historic University City of Heidelberg, first settled by Roman legions.

At the end of our journey, the Kinderdijk windmills and the enchanting canals of Amsterdam bid us goodbye before our return flight home. On future get-togethers we would re-live the highlights and the adventurous events of the historical, discovery-rich European journey.

With feelings of nostalgia and pride, I reflected over the 45 years that had passed since that early and warm February morning, the sun rising over the Caribbean Sea, when a young Argentinean intern had set foot on the Miami tarmac with a heart full of dreams, a strong, unyielding determination, and a rolled-up medical diploma tucked in his suitcase. Most of my dreams had materialized. The setbacks and tragedies had not slackened my pace. I had learned to dance in the rain.

Sometimes it seemed through resolve alone that I had become a successful and respected professional. My contributions to the academic field filled me with humble pride. I knew I had aided numbers of emotionally ill patients. Although not with suture and thread, I had made a difference. My psychiatric patients were the heirs of my desire to heal and make whole, benefiting from my skill and dedicated care in non-invasive procedures. I was a life member of the American Psychiatric Association, a contributing element to the Massachusetts Medical Society, and Director of the Psychiatric Unit at Bon Secours Hospital, in the nearby town of Methuen.

I considered our four children and nine grandchildren to be gifts to my adopted country. They were the legacy of my gratitude for the family's prosperity under the aegis of the security and comfort this land of opportunity had provided. My participation as a covert agent in the Dogwood Chain was a similar expression. As a successful board-certified psychiatrist, lecturer, and world traveler, I attended scientific meetings in a number of countries around the world. Attracting the attention of the Office of Strategic Information, I was recruited and served as an undercover operative. My assignments took me to foreign lands and risky situations where I relied on my wits, learned strategies, and knowledge of human behavior to fulfill varied missions. I willingly participated in a service that was mostly unrewarding, for I seldom knew how my part meshed with the unknown whole, and so, I had little concrete sense of my efforts' value. Still, the efforts seemed small enough recompense for my good fortune.

I sensed it was getting to be time to envision late-life adjustments. Goals for my and Dolores' last chapter were taking shape in my mind.

I had been toying for some time with the prospect of retirement, and tentatively spoke of the possibility of transferring the practice to my part-time psychiatric associate. She had been attracted by the offer. Now, the opportune time seemed to have arrived to enter more serious negotiations.

But finalizing an agreement needed to be postponed as the ringing of wedding bells was again sounding along the green mountains flanking the Mad River Valley in Vermont.

Melissa had met Charles Sisson Barrett Jr., aka CB, on the slopes of Lincoln Peak at Sugarbush, a Vermont ski resort in the town of Warren. Freezing winds and falling snow couldn't chill the mutually warm feelings nestled in their hearts. The relationship progressed through a wholesome romance, flourishing into the decision to share their lives forever.

CB was also a transplant, a non-native Vermonter who had moved to the Green Mountain State drawn by the beauty of its mountains, their challenging snow-covered trails and valleys, and their cold serpentine streams. But mostly by the friendly demeanor of its inhabitants.

Originally from Rhode Island, his family still lived in the Providence area. He was a lover of gourmet cooking, and after demonstrating his skills in entry-level jobs in the food industry, he had worked his way up to the position of executive chef in the well-established and renowned Hyde-Away Inn in the Mad River Valley.

Long distance arrangements were cumbersome to organize, which caused Dolores to travel north on a number of occasions, helping Melissa to choose the venue, lodging accommodations, and church preparations. I had also been an active participant, accompanying Dolores on several trips. This wedding had a special significance in my life. My younger daughter and last child taking her marriage vows had added another branch to the DeNapoli family tree. Eventually, all the steps for the joyous occasion were finalized.

The wedding party comprised of family, relatives, and friends filled the accommodations at the Essex Culinary Resort and Spa situated in the Vermont countryside of Essex Junction, a 15-minute drive from Burlington. A replica of a vintage, motorized San Francisco cable car from the Gay Nineties transported the wedding party to St. Anthony's Church in South Burlington with a sense of nostalgia and flair.

Prior to the final preparations, a meeting of both families had been arranged to discuss particulars of the wedding, especially regarding the religious ceremony. CB's family followed the teachings of the Quaker faith known as the Society of Friends. An amicable agreement having been reached, the ceremony would be held in a Catholic venue.

Melissa and I arrived in a white limousine. On the ride to church, I placed around her wrist a white gold bracelet decorated with delicate Rose of France gems, which I had purchased for this occasion on one of my visits to Buenos Aires. This traditional gesture had started with Deirdre's wedding when I had given her a diamond bracelet on our way to the wedding ceremony.

Once again, beaming with pride, I would give away my other little girl to start her romantic journey with the other most important man in her life.

Following the formal and joyful ceremony, the wedding guests were delighted with a ten-mile trolley excursion trough the Vermont landscape to the reception site, a large function tent on the grounds of the Shelburne Museum, a National Historic landmark on the shores of Lake Champlain. Upon arrival, guests were greeted with cocktails and hors d'oeuvres offered in a garden setting with white tablecloth-covered tables lighted by antique lanterns suspended from surrounding trees. Moving into the function tent, a formal dinner was served to the sound of romantic melodies. Dancing and socializing among the attendees continued until late in the evening. Returning to the Essex Resort, the festal entertainment lasted into the early morning hours.

Dolores and I had accomplished every parent's dream. The children had formed their own families, and grandchildren were adding love and cheerfulness to our daily life.

CHAPTER SIXTEEN

As the pleasant memories of Melissa's wedding receded, I returned my reflections to designing the next chapter of my life. I evaluated my feelings about daily activities: my professional involvement, opportunities for recreation, and remaining goals, some that I had tabled for some time. How would I structure my days if the time to retire had arrived? I knew stimulation for my mind would be a vital necessity. Before I finalized the sale of my practice, I had to be certain that I would be engaged in interesting pursuits that provided a sense of accomplishment. This was my priority. I had witnessed too many depressive responses by patients who had inadequately prepared for their retirement. Whatever had motivated their exit from working life, they'd failed to assess how much time they would have on their hands and how they would fill their days. After just a few months away from life-long employment and routines, individuals, mainly men, become bored because of lack of physical or intellectual stimulation. This boredom eventually leads to feelings of depression and unworthiness.

I was determined to see retirement as an opportunity to pursue interests put aside in busier years. For some time, I had wanted to expand my computer skills and increase my proficiency in French as Dolores was fluent in the language because of her French-Canadian ancestry. I was already fluent in Spanish, could communicate in Italian, and had extensive knowledge of Portuguese and Papiamento, a Creole-based language spoken throughout the islands of the Netherlands Antilles, including Aruba. I also spoke some Guaraní, an indigenous tongue spoken in subtropical Northern Argentina (the second official language of the province of Corrientes), and Paraguay.

There was also my love of world history. Starting in adolescence, I had delved into historic events related to the Roman Republic and my interest on this topic has continued until the present day. As a result of this extensive reading I had accumulated significant knowledge of their culture and social structure. Most enticing to me was learning about the life of Gaius Julius Caesar, the ingenious political and military leader whose successes and tragic demise had set the course for the transition from the Republic to the Roman Empire.

Because of my responsibilities, I had relegated this interest to something I would take up again later; but the fascination with my hero never diminished. Now was the perfect time to return to the questions that history continually prodded me to consider.

Having assured myself that I could be reasonably occupied, my part-time associate, Doctor Gouri Datta and I entered legal negotiations for the purchase and transfer of my psychiatric practice to her. Under the terms reached by agreement, I would continue assisting on a part-time basis for six months, after which time I would fully retire.

With more time available, I enrolled in a nearby community college, taking courses in computer sciences and intermediate French. I then continued with private lessons from a French professor, Madame Maguy Thomson, and joined a French conversational group meeting Saturday mornings in a near-by café. Interacting with my francophone *amis* led to rewarding artistic and literary relationships. A particularly devoted classmate familiarly referred to as *GE*, played a significant role in mentoring me in the intricacies of French grammar, idiomatic expression, and Gallic literature.

To stay current with professional developments and maintain friendships within the medical community, I had also continued my membership in the Aesculapian Club, a physician's group founded in the 1920s. During its monthly meetings in the friendly ambiance of the Lanam Club, a private social club in the Merrimack Valley, the fourteen to twenty physicians attending discussed the latest medical advances as well as inside-hospital happenings, including promotions, interactions, and transgressions of members of the hospital family. My plans also included continuing to attend medical conferences and related functions.

I wanted to stay involved with UNICO, a non-political, non-sectarian charitable organization promoting Italian heritage and culture. The organization offers scholarships to outstanding high school seniors of Italian heritage. It also provides for the needs of others by supporting charitable agencies in the region. I was a charter member of the UNICO Merrimack Valley Chapter, and an active participant as a board of director's officer.

Of course, foremost in my mind were both the long-term love of travel, and the continued undercover service to the nation as an Office of Strategic Information operative.

As my retirement became final, I applied for transfer to the honorary staff of the hospitals I had served, and requested the boards of registration in New Hampshire, New York and Massachusetts to place my medical license on inactive status.

My medical career had come to an end. Throughout the years, I had ardently navigated a road plagued with potholes, bouncing from the unexpectedly dark days of an ill-chosen internship to the heights of prestigious and rewarding achievements in the field of psychiatry. I was satisfied.

The lure of distant skies materialized with a call from Luke offering me participation in a joint assignment across several frontiers in Eastern European countries. Luke had already obtained clearance from his OSI contact, but approval from Mike was mandatory for me to come along on such an undertaking.

The author with a view of Budapest, Hungary behind him.(2006)

The stratagem was simple. Two elderly gentlemen vacationing on a river cruise on the Danube River traversing from Budapest, Hungary to Constanta, a Romanian port city on the Black Sea. The trip included four nights in Prague.

It was an enticing and provocative project. However, there were two hurdles to vault: my governmental confirmation to go-ahead, and convincing Dolores the trip would be a good outlet for Luke's grief. It had been almost a year since Sonia had passed away, losing her battle with pancreatic cancer. This was a necessary quasi-deception I found distasteful. This deception bothered me while my extra-marital liaisons did not, maybe because of ingrained cultural expectations. I wasn't really lying to Dolores. Luke truly needed to process his feelings of loss and begin to move on. I had also come to realize that knowledge of my involvement in OSI operations would have been more difficult for Dolores. It would have created unnecessary concern over my safety. Dolores was sympathetic to my plea and understanding of Luke's need for emotional relief. Weeks went by before Mike called with an affirmative response. By then it was early spring.

At Logan Airport I waited for Luke's plane to arrive from Akron. We had several hours before the flight to Prague and decided to have a light snack and a beer at the airport bar. The layover gave us a chance to update personal and family news, and to familiarize ourselves with the joint assignment. Luke was preoccupied with the safety of the mission. Prague was not of much concern. Having been in the Czech City three other times had allowed me to establish safe connections. Communist rule had terminated years before. The breakup of Czechoslovakia had made the Czech Republic a less dangerous society but still a center for intrigue and clandestine meetings of foreign operatives. Other eastern European countries included in the tour were of greater concern because of unstable governments and their disregard for individual liberties, a residue of years of communist indoctrination.

Front and side view of the Prague astronomical clock.(2006)

The Argentinean embassy in Prague.

Our overnight flight with a London stopover, landed at Ruzine International Airport in Prague early in the morning. We were to join the rest of our tour group at the Dorint Hotel Don Giovanni in the Vinohrady section of the city.

Our first order of business was to make contact with our Czech connection, an agent by the name of Dobrolav. Neither Luke nor I knew the operative's gender. We were waiting in the arrival lounge when a well-dressed young man approached me, extended his hand, and cheerfully offered a greeting, "Professor DeNapoli, welcome to beautiful Prague. My name is Dobrolav." The coded phrase was spoken in accented English.

Dobrolav offered us a ride to the hotel. On the way, we stopped for a mid-morning coffee at the Café Milena in the Old Town Square with a view of the medieval astronomical clock, or Prague Orloj. We conversed freely, but Dobrolav was reticent to release any personal information other than being of Croatian origin.

He centered the conversation around our special assignment in a city a few miles from the small town of Jesenik, near the Polish border, some 150 miles east of Prague. This presented an unexpected logistical problem. The river cruise tour itinerary, organized by the Boston-based World Travel Circle, consisted of four nights in Prague, a transfer to Budapest by bus, with a stop for lunch in Bratislava, capital of Slovakia. Then we were to board a riverboat in Budapest to sail the Danube River to the Black Sea.

In order to carry out our assignment, we would need to break away from the tour group, rent a car and drive to Jesenik, and rejoin the group in Bratislava. We questioned whether the tour director would agree to this arrangement.

After settling into our hotel room, we joined the other tour participants in the function room to meet each other and to be addressed by the program director. He introduced himself as Andrei, a native of Craiova, Romania. He was fluent in English as well as several eastern European languages.

"At the end of the meeting we should approach Andrei," I suggested.

"No, no, not me!" replied Luke, "You are the psychiatrist. You know how to talk to people. It's your job to convince him!"

I just nodded. I would handle it.

"Meet me at the bar," said Luke before I left.

I was back before very long, strolling into the bar with a smirk and feeling superior. "All done. We'll meet them in Bratislava."

"Did he give you a hard time?" Luke wanted to know.

"Not really. We talked about places in Prague, and he realized I was familiar with the city. I also fabricated a story that friends from Argentina living outside of Prague had invited us to spend a couple of days in their home, and then they would drive us to Bratislava."

"Great job! You *are* good!" exclaimed Luke.

"By the way, I gave him hundred dollars. You owe me fifty," I concluded. "You bastard!" muttered Luke, "You bribed him!"

"Well, kind words only go so far," and with a grin I took a sip of my drink.

I had learned in the conversation with Andrei that this was his first year with the World Travel Circle, Romania Office, and he depended heavily on gratuities from tour participants to supplement his salary, which provided for his wife and their 5 year-old son, living in Romania.

Following breakfast the next morning, we rented a car, a Czech-made Skoda Octavia with the help of the hotel concierge. The rental agency provided us with maps and directions to Jesenik. We were thrilled about spending several hours driving through the countryside. It was an enjoyable learning experience to travel across hills covered with lush growth of multicolor wildflowers, small shallow streams of clear water, and large cultivated fields. Most interesting were the Czech people.

After losing our way once or twice, we stopped for directions. Neither Luke nor I spoke the language but managed to communicate with gestures and a few French and Italian words. The *Czech-Hungarian Survival Vocabulary Sheet* included in the tour package was quite helpful.

We met amicable people in the small restaurant-bar, where we stopped for lunch and at the family-owned Inn in Jesenik, where we stayed for the night.

Our contact had arranged a visit to a steel manufacturing plant, introducing us as businessmen in the United States steel industry. We had a chance to inspect their production line and to gather needed information. We had enough time to take a short ride into Polish territory, but fears of being detained for illegal entry made us turn back.

The day-long drive to Bratislava was equally interesting and informative. At the border town of Honodin, border guards stopped us before crossing the Morava River Bridge. They denied us entrance to Slovakia as we did not have the required permit from the rental agency to take the car outside the country's borders. The guards at the check point helpfully clarified the situation with a phone call to the rental agency, allowing us to continue our enjoyable jaunt.

Arriving in Bratislava at dusk we found lodging at the small Hotel Baronka. We were to meet the tour group the next day at the Patronsky Pivovar for lunch and continue with them on the bus to Budapest.

Andrei was ecstatic and relieved when Luke and I entered the restaurant. He shook our hands effusively in welcome. Another thirty or so of our fellow excursionists greeted us with questions about our whereabouts since Prague.

After finishing a meal of typical Slavic fare of pljeskavica (grilled meat), pierogi (mashed potatoes and cheese) and pastrmalija (bread pie), we boarded the motor coach heading south on E73, the international road, for the final 130 miles of the trip.

Arriving at the elegant Corinthia Aquincum Hotel in downtown Budapest we joined with approximately another hundred travelers for the river cruise to the Black Sea. This diverse group included Americans from a number of different states along with British, Germans, Italians, and other Europeans.

Following the reception dinner, the program manager addressed the passengers, dividing us into three smaller groups, with a program director in charge of each one.

Andrei, who had developed a special relationship with us, had listed Luke and me in his group, and for the rest of the tour, he would discuss with us any decisions affecting the group's activities. Embarking on the riverboat was scheduled to take place in two days.

While savoring a drink in the hotel lounge, Andrei approached us. He appeared conflicted and preoccupied, indicating that major changes in the tour's itinerary were to be anticipated. Because of the heavy spring thaw, the waters in the Danube were unusually high, making clearance impossible for the riverboat to navigate under the multiple bridges along the way to the Black Sea.

He confided that the changed plans would also imply changing stops along the route.

The program manager would again address the members in the morning, offering the choice of being flown back to their country of origin or continuing the tour by motor coach. Because of the ulterior purpose of our trip, we opted for continuing by bus, especially since we had a strong ally in Andrei. Unbeknown to us this would entail a disorganized itinerary through uncharted and dangerous territory.

Would the original assignments be modified? The answer rested on our new contact person in Budapest. For the moment waiting was the only option.

Those who opted to continue the tour were moved to the riverboat docked in one of the Pest piers and used as lodging for the three-day stay.

Budapest is two separate cities on opposite sides of the Danube. Buda and Pest stretch out in panoramic view from the terrace at the castle-like Fisherman's Bastion with its fortification's look-out towers. The tour's itinerary included side trips to visit quaint nearby towns such as Szentendre and Verszprem for a Hungarian culinary experience and wine tasting.

The motor coach would board at noon.

While having breakfast in the dining room, Luke was summoned to the front desk to meet a visitor who introduced himself as Ferko, his contact. They asked me to join them. During the brief meeting, Ferko detailed the assignments and risks involved, offering to furnish us with easily concealed pistols to carry for personal protection. Initially we declined the offer. Up to this point, we had never carried weapons.

I had not carried a gun since my days in the Argentinean army and during the time of Peron's overthrow, although I had frequently engaged in target shooting with friends and with my son in Vermont. I was fairly well acquainted with handguns.

"Why should we carry weapons?" I asked. "Is there something you aren't telling us?" "No, no," replied Ferko, "It's just a precaution."

"A precaution against what? Luke interjected. "Are we in danger?

"Just a precaution," repeated Ferko. "You are in a foreign country. Conditions could become unsteady." And without further explanation he turned around and walked away, ending the discussion.

"What a jerk!" spouted Luke.

"Yeah, I know. But he's our contact and we're stuck with him," I replied.

Under pressure from Ferko, we reluctantly agreed to accompany him to a private firing facility where each of us were issued a Russian-made semi-automatic 9 mm Makarov pistol, along with instructions for their use, and the opportunity to practice on the firing range. We were to conceal the weapons on the underside of the bus seat using duct tape to secure them. Luke always carried a roll of tape in all his travels. "Always necessary," he would say. Ferko assured us that he would be waiting in Bucharest at the completion of the tour to retrieve them.

We returned to the riverboat in time to pack and board the motor coach for Osijek in Croatia, our first destination, 120 miles away. While boarding, we noticed Andrei and the driver loading three cases of white Hungarian wine into the luggage compartment.

"This will be a fun trip," commented Luke.

There were 38 passengers in the 62-seat coach. A second bus carried the rest of the group. Another 45 travelers opted to return to their own countries.

Luke and I settled comfortably in the back of the bus where most of the seats were unoccupied. A few other tourists followed us, as in the eyes of the passengers, the independent side trip from Prague and obvious familiarity with Andrei, gave us status as knowledgeable and vaguely privileged passengers.

After a rest stop in the town of Kalocsa, we arrived at the Croatian border. The driver parked the bus near the gate, and he and Andrei walked to the guard house. Thirty minutes later they returned, expressing concern about the demands of the border guards to review, not only passports, but to check everybody's luggage and personal bags. The process would take hours. They would try the strategy of offering them a case of wine if they would check passports only. With the case of wine in hand they walked back to the guard station, and the anxious waiting continued.

About an hour had passed when we saw Andrei, the driver, and a guard walking back. The guard boarded the bus and started to collect passports. Some passengers objected to relinquishing their document, angering the guard who harshly stated, through Andrei acting as an interpreter, that the bus could not enter Croatian territory unless everyone gave him their passports. In the meantime, two other guards with machine guns in hand had moved into position blocking the front of the bus. Tension and worries mounted. The guards did not look friendly or at all concerned with social conventions. The situation was troublesome. We were in the middle of nowhere, wondering whether we should turn back or proceed into unfriendly territory. My main concern was the two pistols hidden under the seats. If discovered, Luke and I could be arrested for smuggling weapons into the country. Not a comforting thought.

Fortunately, I could see Andrei hurrying towards the bus with a triumphant smile, carrying a bag containing the passports. The driver followed him closely.

Andrei was obviously familiar with these situations. He knew the guards' natures, the rules of the game, and how to play his hand. Everybody applauded when he entered the bus.

It was almost dusk when the guards lifted the entrance barrier, allowing the motor coach to cross into Croatia with its relieved passengers. Andrei tried to alleviate our concerns by stressing that Croatians were peaceful, friendly people. The guards had simply been overzealous in their performance of duties or merely hoping for a bribe, which was apparently customary.

His assessment was confirmed when we arrived in Osijek and were received with warm greetings and friendly smiles. Passengers' worries dissipated further after cocktails and an appetizing meal at the hotel.

During the night I woke up, still concerned about the guns, which we had covertly carried to our room. I felt it was riskier to carry them than not having them at all. What were we to do? Shoot our way out of a perilous situation? This was not a movie; it was real life.

Suddenly, I realized the pistols were covered with Luke's and my fingerprints from firing them at the range. I thought of a solution. In the morning I would wipe them clean, and when on the bus I would hide them in the underside of unoccupied seats. Satisfied with the plan, I went back to sleep.

In the morning, I discussed with Luke my concerns and the possible solution. Luke admitted having the same preoccupations.

My suggested approach to the problem seemed reasonable, and Luke handed me his gun.

Looking in the corridor, I saw the maid's cleaning cart. I walked by and took a pair of gloves and a spray bottle of cleaning fluid. Back in the room, with gloves on, I carefully wiped both weapons clean, wrapping them in a newspaper for further disposition. I then hid them in my suitcase.

At breakfast, we noticed that unrest and frustration were spreading rapidly among the group because information was lacking regarding the itinerary and traveling conditions were becoming more uncomfortable. Passengers resented carrying their luggage in and out of the bus, and having to pack and unpack at every stop, basically, living out of their suitcases. Here it was, the second day in Osijek, yet nobody, including Andrei, knew the plans for the next leg of our travels.

Andrei, too, was becoming increasingly frustrated that the tour company's central office was not forthcoming with either clear information or concise directions. Only at the very last minute would Andrei receive instructions as to the next destination and hotel location. He tried to appease the passengers, relying heavily on the cooperation of Luke and me to support his efforts to maintain a cordial environment. Andrei's eyes pleaded for our help. We did what we could to ease the tensions, making light of the situation and telling guests about our exploring the town we were currently in.

That night our departure was announced for the next morning. Belgrade, capital of Serbia, would be our next two-day layover. In the morning I entered the bus minutes ahead of the rest of the group, carrying the package containing the guns. With a Swiss Army knife borrowed from Luke, I made a slit on the underside covering of two seats in the back of the bus, and with gloved hands pushed the two pistols into the opening, where they remained for the rest of our journey.

The palace in Belgrade, Serbia.

The author in Belgrade, Serbia.

The bus departed shortly thereafter with an assembly of unhappy, embittered passengers. The ride was long and tedious with repeated delays due to road construction. To cover the 120 miles to Belgrade, it took close to four hours with a rest stop in Kurmin, a picturesque village a few miles along the way in Serbian territory.

Palace in Belgrade, Serbia.

Government building in Montenegro, Serbia

At the border crossing there was an hour's delay as the passengers were ordered to leave the bus, and then ushered into a large waiting area. In the meantime, Andrei had brought the guards another of the cases of wine as a gesture of friendliness. Tension was high. One by one, the weary travelers were allowed back to the motor coach after each passport had been inspected.

A number of older passengers were beginning to show signs of real distress, aggravated by increasingly warmer and more humid weather. Many regretted their choice of continuing the tour. This was a far cry from the leisurely cruise on the Danube River they had initially paid for. The inconvenience of getting on and off the bus repeatedly, packing and unpacking their suitcases at each hotel, and the constant uncertainty of what came next was no one's idea of a vacation.

The originally scheduled relaxing and captivating river cruise was progressively becoming a nightmarish, disorganized ordeal. We were stuck on a lurching bus with no pre-arranged city tours or visits to cultural, historic, or otherwise interesting locations. Noticed for their absence were welcome dinners, gourmet meals, and lodging in first-rate hotels. Andrei had repeatedly tried to justify the actions of his superiors but was unconvincing. He was the scapegoat for the company's inefficiency; the target of angry remarks and complaints and questions for which he had no satisfactory answers. He was just another victim, as were all in the group, of the insensitive actions of the company's executives and their failure to plan for contingencies.

Luke and I, and a small number of passengers from a church group from Madison, Arkansas occupied the back seats of the bus. The five women and three men, a mother and her grown son among the group, spent their time chatting with us, telling stories and jokes, singing, and making the best of an increasingly calamitous situation.

With sighs of relief all around, we finally reached the Hotel Moskva in the heart of Belgrade. We arrived two days ahead of the original schedule, which meant that Luke and I missed our expected contact person. He or she was supposed to give us the necessary instructions about future assignments.

Andrei had hinted that the next destination might be the city of Sofia, the capital of Bulgaria, taking us even further away from the planned locations.

Luckily for Andrei and for the rest of us, Belgrade was a scheduled stop on the original itinerary. Proper arrangements had been made and all passengers had been pre-registered at the Hotel Moskva. Room assignments were smoothly distributed. The evening meal was a gourmet's delight, and later, Serbian performers clad in folk costumes danced and sang traditional music to entertain us.

Tomb of Josip Broz Tito in the House of Flowers, Sofia, Bulgaria.

Over the next two days, visits to Pionirski Park, Kalemegdan, the older part of the city with its historic Citadel on the crest of a hill, a fortress dating from Roman times, and the St. Sava Orthodox Cathedral, the second largest in the world built in 1989, helped assuage our fellow travelers' annoyances over past inconveniences. A reminder of the rise and fall of socialistic Yugoslavia was evoked by a visit to ex-dictator Tito's Mausoleum and the House of Flowers, the resting place of the benevolent dictator, Josip Broz, aka Tito.

Some of our shared discontent had dissipated as result of the fine reception and interesting views of this Serbian capital on the Danube River. The change, however, would be short lived. At breakfast on the morning of departure, Andrei informed the group that World Travel Circle had arranged for the tour to continue on to Sofia, capital of Bulgaria, some 250 miles away.

The news was received with grunts of disapproval. All of us anticipated a day-long, tiresome ride with nothing to see, traveling motorways and bumpy, back roads through the Serbian plains and on through the mountainous entry into Bulgaria. The passengers showed their discontent with a chorus of complaints about the unscheduled itinerary.

A rest stop two hours later on the outskirts of Aleksinac, a small village off route E73, aggravated the temperaments of the tourists still further. In the small gas station and variety store, we had to stand in line for almost 15 minutes to use the restrooms, and equally as long at the check-out counter to buy soft drinks and snacks.

The rest of the journey was a blend of discomfort and boredom plus the usual aggravation of the delay at the border crossing. We were not a happy group. It was still daylight when we entered the downtown area of Sofia, greeted by bleak block-housing; reminders of the socialist-era, and Russian-style communist architecture.

But while roaming around the city during our three-day stay, Luke and I discovered neighborhoods with tree-lined boulevards and sidewalk cafes, aristocratic 19th century European-style buildings, and ancient Byzantine Orthodox Churches. Women in traditional costumes sold flowers on street corners, and folk musicians serenaded passersby.

At night after dinner, we would meet in the lounge of the Hotel Lozenetz where we were staying. Between shots of Jagermeister, a German herbal liqueur, the conversation centered on the interesting discoveries we had turned up in our wandering of the city's streets.

Leaving for Bucharest the next day the travelers were in a more relaxed mood. We had anticipated that the three-day, originally scheduled stay would be smoother, and looked forward to our flight home after the ordeal of the poorly organized motor-coach trip. Many expressed their intentions of avoiding future traveling with World Travel Circle.

The landscape had changed as we drove, leading us through green plains, past lazily flowing streams and flowering meadows. One hundred and forty-five miles later, we arrived in the town of Svishtov on the south bank of the Danube, a former Roman colony that acted as the base of war campaigns against Barbarian tribes long ago. After the required rest stop, the bus boarded the ferry crossing to Zimnicea, Romania, continuing the remaining 90 miles to Bucharest.

I was more than glad to leave behind all the unpleasant experiences and inconveniences. We traveled the land of Spartacus, the slave from Thrace, who led the uprising against the Roman Republic in 73 BC. My mind wandered through history as we covered the landscape of today's southwest Bulgaria. Because of the superimposition of the two time periods, it was an enjoyable ride, as much for the adventuring of my imagination through the lore of Spartacus as for traversing green plains and networks of rivers descending from the Carpathian Mountains.

The spiritual, intellectual and material accomplishment of historic heroes had an integral significance on my journey through life. They strengthened my confidence and determination to reach my goals and taught me to make the best of any situation.

Arriving in Bucharest, we were lodged at the Hotel Sofitel in Montreal Square. In the lobby, while retrieving our luggage, I suddenly remembered the guns concealed under the seats of the bus. I walked outside post-haste. Fortunately, the bus was still parked in front of the hotel. I removed the pistols and tucked them under my belt, covered by the jacket I was wearing. Once in the room, I hid them in the suitcase.

Why am I the one in charge of these god-damned guns? I swore, *This is Luke's mission. If we had needed to be armed at some point, wouldn't Luke have had to worry about the guns?* It was my fault. I was always the one to step up and take the risk.

That evening Luke received a call from Ferko, arranging a meeting at a small secluded restaurant overlooking the Grozavesti Bridge. A feeling of relief passed through my body when I handed Ferko the paper bag containing the burdensome pistols. Who had decided we should be armed had remained unclear. We also never learned the value of the information we reported.

The next assignment presented by Ferko was simple, but no less important than the ones we had conducted at the aircraft factory and the iron ore mine in Bulgaria.

We headed for the Palace of Parliament, headquarters of the International Conference Center, and second largest construction project after the Pentagon. It was rumored that the Palace had an extensive anti-nuclear bunker for governmental emergency use. Our mission was to gain access to the Palace, and if possible, to the bunker. However, we had to settle for only a visit to the impressive Palace lobby.

The next day a city tour bused the group to the National Museum of Art, the Central University, the majestic Patriarchal Cathedral, and the Plata Universitati, a memorial square for the heroes of the 1989 revolution against communist rule.

On my own, I made a visit to the Carol Davila University of Medicine, the largest health sciences institution in Romania, founded in 1857 by Carol Davila, a French expatriate physician.

Two days later, we left Bucharest, the city sprawled on both banks of the Dambovita River, on route to Otopeni International Airport, 10 miles away.

There, Luke and I boarded a British Airline's jet leaving for London to catch a connecting flight to Boston. Arriving at Logan Airport on a starry spring evening, we relaxed into feelings of pride and accomplishment despite the trip's many disruptions. How our collected information would be used we might never know, but we had fulfilled our mission together.

I waited until Luke's flight was ready for departure for Akron, waving goodbye as he passed through the security check station.

On the bus ride home to Amesbury, I reflected on my relationship with Luke. Our friendship dated back to the first meeting in Aruba years ago. From the first moment, we felt a strong attachment; more than friends, we felt like brothers. We could understand each other without resorting to verbal communication. We could read each other's thoughts and complement our actions with just a directive look. We were a formidable team.

It would have been good to have met much earlier, while we were younger, I wished we had. I felt content that our closeness and support for each other in contrasting moments of delight and concerned risk had not only further cemented our relationship but had help him to successfully resolve residual feelings of loss and loneliness.

CHAPTER SEVENTEEN

Now fully retired, I pursued recreational and social activities with a certain degree of anxiety. I was determined to keep my social calendar filled worried that otherwise my retirement might not go well.

Weekly French lessons, conversational French meetings, and computer classes occupied most days of my week. Monthly medical conferences, UNICO Board of Directors and members' dinner meetings, the Italian charitable organization, and outings with friends kept my social agenda busy.

Family get-togethers including short trips to Rhode Island and Vermont to visit Melissa and Tiki, and participation in our grandchildren's school-related and recreational activities left no time for boredom.

We were due for a trip to Argentina. The plan was to leave sometime in the fall of 2006 from Boston's Logan Airport, and arrive in New York's JFK an hour later. After a three-hour layover, we would board an American Airline's jet for the almost eleven-hour non-stop flight to Buenos Aires. The trip would be more comfortable now than the first time I made it, but the intervening years had dampened my enthusiasm for flying such long distances. Only the anticipation of being with relatives and dear friends would make the long and tiresome journey tolerable and quasi-enjoyable.

With all the arrangements in place, we left home on a gorgeous mid-October afternoon. New England's frosty paint brush had tinged the foliage with a symphony of bright yellow, red and brown colors. Within the next day, nature would change her vestments for us to green leaves and budding flowers as springtime arrived in the Southern Hemisphere.

We spent most of the layover at JFK waiting in line at the security check. Once in flight, after the plane reached cruising altitude, flight attendants served us dinner, and we watched a movie. The cabin lights dimmed after the meal for the passengers to rest and catch some sleep for the remaining hours of the night.

The excitement of returning home, even for so short a vacation, kept me awake. Dolores dozed next to me. Thinking ahead, I anticipated a smooth passage through the immigration check point in contrast with the difficulties I encountered on another trip to Buenos Aires in October of 1982. When we arrived back then, passengers were guided to the immigration station where Dolores presented her American passport, which the immigration officer stamped with the entry date without delay, and she had been allowed to pass through the checkpoint. Behind her, I showed my American passport, which recorded Argentina as my place of birth. The immigration officer examined the passport and ordered me into another office where I was presented with a document to sign that stipulated that I could be subject drafted into the Army.

The Islas Malvinas (Falkland Islands) conflict ended in June of 1982. The military junta ruling the country enacted a new law whereby all nationals residing abroad, when returning to their homeland, were subject to possible drafting into the military if under the age of 55. I was 51. Even though I was a naturalized U.S. citizen, under Argentinean law I was still considered a citizen of Argentina and therefore governed by the laws of the country when within its borders. Being a medical doctor meant I could be commissioned as a medical officer.

I was unwilling to sign such an agreement but being informed that I could not enter the country unless I complied, I reluctantly acquiesced. In the meantime, Dolores sat in the waiting area in a state of extreme apprehension. She sighed with relief as she saw me coming toward her. Briefly I explained the circumstances of the delay, leaving the details to be discussed later.

In the lobby we spotted my sister Nora and her husband Raul anxiously waiting as most of the passengers had already exited. On the drive to Nora's place I gave them a full account of the incident.

Dolores was greatly concerned that I might be drafted or not allowed to leave the country. She insisted that we should consult with the American Embassy in Buenos Aires. There, disappointment permeated our mood when we were informed that, unfortunately, the U.S. Embassy couldn't intervene as I was a native Argentinean.

I tried to alleviate her worries and convince her that it would be no problem for me to flee the country. Long ago, during my basic military training at a base in the Province of Corrientes near the Brazilian border, draftees were not allowed to leave Argentinean soil. However, when on weekend furloughs, many recruits would hire a small motorboat in one of the villages on the Argentinean banks of the Uruguay River, and cross into Brazilian territory to visit the bordellos in Brazil, where there was better entertainment and prices were much lower.

My plan was simple. Dolores could fly on her own to return home to the U.S., while I would cross the river into Brazil, make my way to a large city like Porto Alegre or Sao Paulo, and board a plane to the United States. Fortunately, the plan never needed to be implemented as I was never drafted.

I was brought back from remembering this worrisome trip by the flight attendant serving breakfast. A while later we landed at Ezeiza International Airport on the outskirts of Buenos Aires.

The vacation fulfilled all our expectations: dining out with family and friends, the operas, symphonies, the theater, and quiet evenings with Nora and Raul reliving childhood events. Walking the streets of the old neighborhood, meeting with hospital friends, and army buddies, refreshed old memories.

On the return flight my eyes were moist with tears as our plane bound for New York climbed above the clouds, the night lights of Buenos Aires fading in the distance.

Back home, I became reabsorbed into the routine of daily activities, but remained always on alert for new ventures. Months had gone by with nothing exciting happening when finally, I received a call from Mike on my cell phone. He sounded different. There was a ring of cheerfulness in his voice. He had flown in from Washington and wanted to arrange a meeting. We agreed to get together at the White Eagle Café in Lowell the next day.

Mike's demeanor was different from his usual business-like attitude. He appeared friendlier, and there was a twinkle brightening his eyes. He mainly wanted to discuss the details of the next assignment. When he mentioned Russia, my mind jumped to alert, picturing mean looking armed soldiers, tanks rolling down Red Square, parades of ICBM's, and the sarcastic smiles of communist leaders.

Mike's description of early 2000's friendly relations with the Kremlin and the surge of tourism between both countries toned down the movie that had been playing through my mind. I asked about the possibility of Luke joining me on the assignment. Mike said he would need to consult with his superiors and would then get back to me. With a smile playing across his face, he switched the conversation to his personal life. He had reached the age of 67 and had already applied for retirement from Government Service, effective as of the end of September.

He and his wife anticipated moving back to their hometown of Chandler, Arizona, a suburb of Phoenix. To my surprise, he took a business card out of his wallet, wrote his address on the back, and handed it to me. The card read, D…L…, and gave a Washington, D.C. address. I finally knew Mike's real name.

"If you're ever in Arizona, come visit me," he said. "It will be a pleasure," I responded.

Mike then reverted to the conversation about the upcoming mission.

"You'll be joining a cultural delegation on a river cruise from Moscow to St. Petersburg, with a few stops in between," he informed me. Then he outlined the nature of my mission. "I'll meet you for debriefing on your return," he finished.

"Please, let me know if Luke can accompany me on this assignment," I reminded him. We shook hands and departed.

The next morning at the breakfast table, I casually brought up the subject of a possible river cruise vacation in Russia, from Moscow to St. Petersburg, stopping at Uglish, Yaroslavl, Kizhi, and Svirstroi. Dolores did not find the idea appealing. "I don't feel that Russia is a place I want to go," she commented. "Why don't you call Luke and see if he's interested? You two make a good pair," she concluded. She frequently referred to us as the *odd couple.*

I was surprised by her response. *Was she aware of the secondary motivation of the trip? Had she suspected my undercover work during these past years?* She had never hinted at any knowledge of my clandestine activities, but on occasion she overlooked obvious clues. *Was this purposely done or just an oversight?*

Under the oath of secrecy, I was not at liberty to discuss the subject with Dolores. It was better to leave my questions unanswered. It seemed amazing to have a part of my life as an adjunct to my primary reality. I knew this lifestyle would have been impossible for many.

Two weeks later Mike notified me that Luke would be contacted and might possibly be joining me. After meeting with his agent, Luke readily agreed to the joint venture.

World Circle Company in Boston organized the river cruise. The itinerary began with a four-day stay in Moscow, and then embarked downriver on a boat navigating the Volga River on to St. Petersburg. Side trips to Tallinn, capital of Estonia, and across the Baltic Sea to Helsinki, capital of Finland, would round out the excursion. We would depart on August fourth.

Upon arrival at Moscow International Airport, the group was bused to the Suschevsky Hotel. A tour of the city the next day included the Victory Museum, commemorating the Soviet participation in World War II and the years of the Cold War. The museum was located in the heart of Moscow, capital of the Russian Federation.

On the way to the museum, views of a modern and vibrant city quickly dissipated the residue of negative impressions in my mind gleaned from obviously slanted media reports.

Magnificent modern architecture, wide avenues traveled by late model cars, lush parks decorated with an abundance of flowers, and colorful onion-domed churches reformed my notions of Moscow into that of a wealthy metropolis stretching along both banks of the Moskva River.

We had visited most parts of the museum, and I was trailing behind the rest of our group of tourists. Luke had disappeared from sight. Suddenly, his unmistakable soft whistle caught my attention. I looked around and spotted him leaning over the third-floor marble banister above me, at the top of the sweeping white marble staircase, gesturing for me to come up. When I reached the third level, I discovered that he had managed to open the locked entrance to another large exhibit that was not accessible to the general public.

Luke always prided himself that no locked barrier could trump him.

He guided me to the exhibit showing the remnants of the U-2 spy plane that was allegedly shot down by a soviet missile at an altitude of about 70,000 feet on May 1st, 1960, while flying reconnaissance over Soviet territory during the height of the Cold War. A plaque clearly displayed the name Francis Gary Powers and the date. We were unable to decipher the rest of the text written in Russian cyrillic script.

At first glance, the wreckage seemed not to display any burned parts. An intact ejection seat was by its side. In the amateur opinions of Luke and me, it resembled more the result of a crash-landing rather than being struck by a missile. Apparently, almost 50 years after the event, the U-2 incident still harbored questions engendering scrutiny.

I was taking pictures with my small disposable Kodak camera when abruptly interrupted by a loud, "NO PICTURES!" in heavily accented English. An armed guard had entered the area. We had been caught read handed! Waving his rifle, he gestured for me to hand over the camera, which I had quickly slipped into the pocket of my light summer jacket. My heart started pounding, but I tried to maintain my composure. Meekly I handed the camera to the rifle-toting guard. I wondered if this time was going to be it. My last...Visions of jail or worse, flooded my mind. Pointing to my identification card, I attempted to explain that I was a tourist with the World Travel Circle, but he didn't understand English. He ushered us out of the large third-floor hall, the door of which bore a "Restricted Area – Authorized Personnel Only" sign written in Russian, later translated by our tour guide.

Descending the white marble staircase followed by the guard, Luke lamented under his breath, "Too bad about the pictures." Softly and trying to force a smile I replied, "I gave him the other camera," a tactic learned during training at Headquarters. "Always carry an extra camera and cell phone for emergencies," frequently warned other more experienced agents.

To our surprise and great relief, the armed guard allowed us to rejoin our tour group without any further consequences. My hands were cold and sweaty, but we had weathered the ordeal. Luke and I had accomplished 'step one' of our assignment as undercover operatives. Reunited with the rest of the group, we returned to the hotel.

The next day would be another challenging experience with a visit to the space center, step two of our mission. Luke and I had been quite excited anticipating this tour-site located a few miles outside the city. From classified U.S. reports we were aware of the advanced Russian technology and their successful accomplishments in space exploration. However, much of the Russian's programs had never been published.

Traveling through the suburbs of Moscow treated us to flowering gardens, the tree-lined roads of the countryside, and the architectural style of the *dachas*; summer residences of affluent city dwellers.

Sliding iron gates marked the entrance to the center. After the required stop at the security station, the bus headed for the parking area, the starting point of the walking tour. I could see the disappointed expression on Luke's face, perhaps not very different from my own. We were headed towards a number of old and rundown warehouse-type buildings.

A guard from the security detail was our English-speaking guide. We visited two of the buildings housing remnants of space capsules and personal survival equipment dating back to the infancy of space technology, a museum-type display with minimal military or political significance.

A conference had been arranged to meet former astronauts who would share their experiences and answer questions from the visitors. Actually, only one retired cosmonaut was present, communicating through an interpreter.

During the question and answer phase of the presentation, Luke boldly asked, "How many astronauts lost their lives in the initial stages of space exploration?"

The retired astronaut's startled expression of annoyance clearly indicated that he actually understood the question in English. He hurriedly exchanged an angry-sounding, gruff conversation in Russian with the translator whose curt reply was, "classified information." Well, we were not there to make friends. The entire visit had been boring and disappointing. We had envisioned a tour of something like the Astro Space Center-Levedev Physics Institute in the City, or the Pushchino Astrophysics Observatory in Pushchino-on-Oka, an hour's drive from Moscow, both sites on our assignment list.

To the program director's objections, Luke and I always acted independently, either selecting which arranged tours to take, or exploring the city on our own. We wandered for miles through streets and avenues, riding the subway system or boarding buses to the end of the line and back. We enjoyed the spectacular appearance of the metro stations with their long steep escalators, marble walls, ornate chandeliers, mosaics, and murals. We walked Tverskaya Street with its variety of shops and outside cafes, and discovered the Chocolate Factory with multiple chocolate reproductions of famous world structures: animals, transportation vehicles, and all sorts of other objects. We entered the magnificent lobby of the Moscow Ritz Carlton Hotel, one of the most elegant hotel entrances I have ever seen in my world traveling. Outside a line of luxurious BMWs, Mercedes Benzes, Ferraris, Jaguars and Porsches waited for privileged hotel guests.

Tired and thirsty, we looked for a place to enjoy a cold beer when we spotted a bar-like establishment named "Oregon КАЗИНО".

"Maybe it's owned by some guy from Oregon, USA," joked Luke.

We entered and discovered that it was actually a casino, though nothing like the ones at home. We saw no blackjack or craps tables, but there were numerous slot and poker playing machines, and other games totally unfamiliar to us.

After enjoying a couple of beers at the bar, and surprisingly, fried chicken wings, Luke decided to play a poker machine. Less than an hour later we left with Luke pocketing a wad of Rubles equivalent to approximately 500 dollars. Generously, he paid for our consumption at the bar.

We spent time in Red Square visiting Lenin's Tomb, and St. Basil Cathedral, and did some souvenir shopping at the famous GUM Department Store. An interesting experience was visiting the Kremlin, a triangular-shaped fortress in the center of town, site of government offices, seventeenth and nineteenth century palaces, transient residences of Peter the Great and other tsars. We passed historical golden-domed cathedrals, churches, and the Ivan the Great Bell Tower. On our route was the

National Armory, the Kremlin Palace, and the Senate Building which housed President Vladimir Putin's office. All buildings were heavily guarded by armed soldiers.

Contrary to our expectations, most official buildings were closed to visitors. "No significant information to gather here!" I commented.

As was the norm in previous trips, at night we gathered at the hotel's lounge with the other tour participants. They wanted to hear Luke and I relate adventures and discoveries during our explorations of the city.

Four days after our arrival in Moscow, the tour passengers boarded the *Tikhi-Don* river boat to navigate the Volga-Baltic Waterway, which would pass through 18 locks before entering the Neva River and docking in St. Petersburg. On the way

Above left: Tomb of Lenin on right and the Kremlin behind the wall.
Above right and top of next page: The Kremlin (2007)

we would stop in Uglish, Goritsi, Kishi Island, and Svirstroy. We would also stop at small villages with unusual church architecture, the home of Valentina Tereshkova the first soviet woman cosmonaut, Chaika watches, and a vendor's paradise for souvenirs, Russian dolls, and hand-crafted jewelry.

Wooden carved churches on Kizhi Island, Russia. (2007)

After twelve days on Russian rivers, we arrived in St. Petersburg, known as the *Venice of the North,* with more than 300 bridges adorned with statues, obelisks and wrought iron railings. The bridges crossed rivers and canals to connect its more than 40 islands. Bused to the Ambassador-Baltic Hotel, we settled into our room and were greeted by the charm and style of the Old Empire.

Roaming around this city of myth and mystery, we admired the Alexander Column in the center of Palace Square marking the Russian victory over Napoleon, the famous Bronze Horsemen in Senate Square (monument to Peter the Great), and The Hermitage with its Winter Palace (the Royal residence of the Tsars).

Moored in front of the Naval Academy, we visited The Aurora, a cruiser in the Russo- Japanese War, known for its role in the 1917 Bolshevik Revolution, now a popular museum.

Having visited our fair share of religious places, we purposely bypassed churches, cathedrals and synagogues. We did not fail to sample 'blinys' (Russian pancakes), and the popular strong vodka at the Café-Club Arka, around the corner from the hotel.

The bridge over the Neva River in St. Petersburg, known as the Venice of the North.

Government building, St. Petersburg.

Tikhi Ton river boat on the Volga; Yaroslavl, Russia.

238

Monastery in Yaroslavl, Russia. (2007)

The three-day stay had not been enough to appreciate the beauty and history of the legendary *City of the Tsars*, but commitment to our mission prompted us to board the motor coach to Tallinn, capital of Estonia, as planned.

After a quick view of Toompea Hill and the Old Town with its two-block-long string of flower kiosks, we moved on to complete our mission. Separating from the tour group, we visited a metallurgic factory near the town of Rapla, which produced heavy armor plates for army vehicles.

Night life at Tallinn overflowed with loudly ebullient Finns attracted by the favorable exchange of Euros to Estonian kroons and the abundance of restaurants, bars, and entertainment.

A view of the Old City in Tallinn, Estonia. (2007)

Blocks of flower shops in Estonia.

The quiet City of Helsinki lay in a sharp contrast 90 minutes away by the *Super Sea Cat* across the Baltic Sea. The seaport capital of Finland was the last stop for us before the flight home. The main attraction in Helsinki was Mannerheim, its main street with the Sokos and Forum shopping malls. We visited Stockmann's, the large department store, though shopping could not be the thrust of our time in the city. Our mission was to concentrate on the metal and engineering industrial complexes surrounding it. We were to assess their production systems, and manufacturing techniques following guidelines learned during an instructional seminar prior to leaving home.

Government building in Helsinki, Finland. (2007)

Satisfied with our accomplishments we boarded the British Boeing 767 for the flight to Heathrow Airport with a sigh of contentment.

We had been comfortably relaxing on the reclined seats of the aircraft's business class when approached by the flight attendant.

"Sir, may I offer you a drink?"

"Ah, yes, thank you," I replied. "I'll have a Tanqueray martini on the rocks, dry, with three olives, in a snifter, please."

CHAPTER EIGHTEEN

Life had been like white water rafting: rough and risky at times, but exciting and rewarding overall. Growing older had not meant slowing down. Like Don Quixote of La Mancha, I was still "reaching for the unreachable star."

With our circle of friends, I had enjoyed sharing some of the amusing happenings of my journey since leaving my native Argentina, keeping to myself sorrowful events and very personal occurrences.

On numerous occasions, friends and others suggested that I record my many anecdotes and experiences. I mentally dismissed the suggestions, arguing that my proficiency in English was not up to the level of literary standards required. Besides, my time was limited due to my involvement in community, social, and intellectual activities. I preferred to live life rather than write about it. Still, the possibility of such a project had always inhabited space in my mind. But now as never before time seemed to move on more rapidly.

It had been almost a year since the debriefing that followed our Russian trip. Mike hadn't been in my thoughts until an invitation arrived from the American Psychiatric Association to participate in a three-day, multidisciplinary seminar in September of 2008, organized by the Scottsdale Psychiatry Society. According to the arrangements, I would be staying at the Arizona-Biltmore-Phoenix Hotel, approximately 20 miles from Mike's home in the city of Chandler.

It would certainly be an excellent opportunity to pay him a visit. I hesitated about calling him in advance or waiting until I was settled in the hotel in Phoenix. I opted for the latter. Mike was surprised and delighted to receive the phone call. He promptly invited me to dinner at his home the following evening, offering to pick me up at the hotel.

We drove to Mike's home on North Dobson Road, a Spanish style house with portico columns and red-tile roof. His wife Rhonda met us at the front door, greeting me with a smile and a friendly, "Welcome to our home. My husband has frequently mentioned your name." She spoke with a noticeable southern drawl despite the many years spent living in Washington.

We had an exquisite home-cooked meal interrupted only by the friendly exchange of family information and post-retirement activities and plans.

I learned that Mike had been a police officer in town before attending Arizona State University, graduating with a law enforcement and political science degree. Moving to Washington, he had been recruited by the CIA, joining the School of Intelligence Analysis. Years later he was transferred to the Office of Strategic Information.

Rhonda and Mike had two married sons living in Virginia, and were the grandparents of five grandchildren. Since his retirement, Mike had been a volunteer for the local school district, teaching courses in personal safety.

It was an intense and effusive reunion. Owing to the many years engaged in clandestine activities, we had a trusting, mutually respectful relationship.

We agreed to meet for lunch at the hotel the next day, to be followed by a short tour of the Sedona Valley to admire the impressive landscape with its red sandstone formations. After that luncheon, we parted with a strong handshake, an amicable hug, and a commitment to stay in touch.

A week before Christmas 2008, I placed a call to Mike to wish him and Rhonda a Merry Christmas and happiness for the coming year. Rhonda answered the phone and to my disbelief tearfully informed me that Mike had passed away four weeks before of a sudden massive heart attack. I was overwhelmed with feelings of sadness and loss. I extended my condolences. Tears of sorrow filled my eyes.

Dwelling with fondness over the relationship with Mike, and the long years of mutual undercover work, I realized that the secret chapter of my life had come to its conclusion. When announcing his retirement, Mike indicated that another agent would contact me regarding future assignments. However, I never again heard from the Office of Strategic Information.

More than a year had passed when I was surprised to receive a *Certificate of Nomination* stating: "For outstanding service and loyalty to the United State of America ... this certifies that Jorge DeNapoli has met the strict requirements set forth by the Congress of the United States, and shall thereby be accepted for Official Membership in The American Legion."

This honor is reserved for those who have serve in the U.S. armed forces.

I could not think of anyone responsible for having submitted my name, but perhaps Mike did this as his last expression of recognition and friendship.

The question would remain unanswered.

EPILOGUE

In the year following Mike's death I re-examined the past and appraised my future. Reflecting on the length of the two hemispheres I had traveled and the breadth of cultures that had opened before me as I emerged from my Argentinean mindset onto the world's stage, I wondered if the story of my journey were distilled, how the spirit of my life's essence might linger on one's palate.

Could my experiences be enjoyed in a snifter with friends, or remain as the wine of my own vintage for my children and grandchildren to sample, hoping they would appreciate its bouquet? Were my language skills adequate, and my memory sufficient to portray my adventures successfully? Could I convey the caprice that risk-taking had afforded, and the jarring dust encountered on my bumpy road? Would they see how I appreciated my gifts: parents wise enough to convey the efficacy of learning as a personal goal, my sense of family, the determination and stamina, and perhaps the luck of being born under the Southern Cross? Was telling all my last challenge to embrace the essence of my being?

On a still, warm, early, autumn afternoon, I gazed at the leaves dancing with the wind already turning to the fire of their true colors. I watched them swirl outlined against the choppy waters of the Merrimack River as it raced to the sea. I daydreamed again of the shadows Roman history cast on my life.

How different was my tall figure from Caesar's at the Rubicon's waters-edge, deciding once more if I should cross?

If I excavated the facts and confronted the meaning of my life's choices, would that change them? How would my accounting of personal and material accomplishments be measured? Would the risk of being misinterpreted be worth the opportunity to share my astonishment and wonder, to possibly even be understood?

I wondered if the joy of Dolores, our children and grandchildren gifted through our marriage would be tarnished by my candor.? Gleefully witnessing them well set on their own paths, satisfied beyond imagining, showered with exuberance, beauty, and contentment of finding significance within the panorama of humanity… could I do it all justice? I had weighed everything carefully, sought some help, and without hesitation crossed my 'Rubicon.' I was comfortable letting my story be told as it had been lived.

The thought of a great man had companioned my resolve:

"I don't measure a man's success by how high he climbs, but how high he bounces when he hits bottom."
~General George S. Patton, Jr. 1885 – 1945

On a crispy evening in the early spring of 2014, Dolores's soul left for her eternal haven to be reunited with our son's. By her side, holding her hand I could feel her life ebbing. The soft crying of our children surrounding her bed, was a painful parting song. Her valiant three-year struggle with a progressive deteriorating pulmonary disease was finally over.

Weeks before, she had finished reading the initial draft of *The Unintentional Immigrant*. The only one of family and friends to do so.

Contrary to my anticipation of a critical response, in particularly because of my sometimes unorthodox behavior, to my surprise and delight, Dolores's comments were supportive and encouraging. Mostly quoting from my own words, she said, "Our journey has certainly been pelted with turbulent events, but I am glad that I was at your side to dance in the rain. We have had a happy life together with many rewarding gifts. Let's look forward to a long peaceful enjoyment of our retirement years."

On a clear starry night, if you carefully search the western sky, you might discover two small brilliant stars close together as if holding hands… or maybe it is just my imagination.

Eventually, a third star, mine, will join them. It might be the last adventure of this "Unintentional Immigrant."

ADDENDUM

Idlewild International Airport was renamed John F. Kennedy International Airport in 1963.

Harlem Hospital, today known as Harlem Hospital Center, has been a teaching hospital affiliated with Columbia University since 1962. In 1969 it underwent major renovations with the construction of the Martin Luther King, Jr. Pavilion, and more recently the Mural Pavilion.

Added specialty services and a more academically oriented medical staff have significantly improved the level of patient care.

Gardner State Hospital closed in 1975. The site is now occupied by The North Central Correctional Institution of Massachusetts.

Middletown State Hospital was renamed Middletown Psychiatric Center and closed permanently in 2006.

Baldpate Hospital has changed its psychiatric orientation. Its emphasis today is in alcohol/drug detox care and rehabilitation.

The Community Savings Bank of Lawrence was acquired by the Andover Savings Bank of Andover, Massachusetts.

Hale Hospital built a brand-new facility nearby that was renamed Merrimack Valley Hospital, still located in the city of Haverhill.

Bon Secours Hospital is still operating under the name of Holy Family Hospital.

R.F. O'Connor & Associates closed during the 1988 recession.

Aunt Julia passed away after a short illness in October of 2013. She was 98 years old.

ABOUT THE AUTHOR

A native of Argentina, author Jorge H. DeNapoli graduated from the University of Buenos Aires Medical School and trained to be a surgeon at the Juan A. Fernandez Hospital in Buenos Aries, Argentina. He arrived in the United States in 1956 for a medical internship. Unable to pursue a surgical career, he became a board-certified psychiatrist trained at the Psychiatric Center in Middletown, New York, the Columbia University Psychiatric Institute, and the Vanderbilt Clinic at the Columbia University-Presbyterian Hospital in New York City.

Dr. DeNapoli opened a private practice in Massachusetts in 1968 for the treatment of anxiety and stress-related disorders, specializing in the interpretation of human behavior. He was the Director of the Psychiatric Unit at Holy Family Hospital in Methuen, Massachusetts and a psychiatric consultant at Lawrence General Hospital in Lawrence, Massachusetts. He was also a psychiatric consultant at Andover Phillips Academy in Massachusetts,.

A life member of the American Psychiatric Association, now retired, the author resides in the Merrimack Valley in Massachusetts, and is an active member of several professional and charitable organizations.

Made in the USA
Middletown, DE
17 November 2019

78881089R00150